ESSENTIAL
FISH

by Alyssa Krekelberg

CONTENT CONSULTANT

Dr. Jessica Arbour
Professor of Biology
Middle Tennessee State University

ESSENTIAL
ANIMALS

Essential Library

An Imprint of Abdo Publishing
abdobooks.com

abdobooks.com

Published by Abdo Publishing, a division of ABDO, PO Box 398166, Minneapolis, Minnesota 55439. Copyright © 2022 by Abdo Consulting Group, Inc. International copyrights reserved in all countries. No part of this book may be reproduced in any form without written permission from the publisher. Essential Library™ is a trademark and logo of Abdo Publishing.

Printed in the United States of America, North Mankato, Minnesota.
102021
012022

Cover Photos: Gaid Kornsilapa/Shutterstock Images (tang); DJ Mattaar/Shutterstock Images (butterflyfish); Jim Agronick/Shutterstock Images (shark); Shutterstock Images (mandarin fish), (fighting fish); Mark Doherty/Shutterstock Images (porcupinefish)
Interior Photos: Mark Doherty/Shutterstock Images, 1; Thomas Lenne/Shutterstock Images, 4; Valery Evlakhov/Shutterstock Images, 5; Red Line Editorial, 7, 50, 102–103; Shutterstock Images, 9, 13, 18, 35, 44, 45, 49, 60, 70, 76, 87, 95, 103 (barracuda), 103 (great white), 103 (mandarin fish), 103 (fighting fish); Greg Brave/Shutterstock Images, 10; Nantawat Chotsuwan/Shutterstock Images, 12, 102 (gar); Charlotte Bleijenberg/Shutterstock Images, 14; Gaid Kornsilapa/Shutterstock Images, 16, 102 (tang); Ethan Daniels/Shutterstock Images, 17, 92, 103 (whale shark); Arunee Rodloy/Shutterstock Images, 20, 102 (catfish); Aleron Val/Shutterstock Images, 21; M. Huston/Shutterstock Images, 22–23; Jeff Rotman/Science Source, 24, 25, 38–39, 47, 96, 102 (skate), 103 (tuna); Gilbert S. Grant/Science Source, 27; Tristan Tan/Shutterstock Images, 28, 102 (eel); Dante Fenolio/Science Source, 30; Mark Bowler/Science Source, 31; Francesco Ricciardi/Shutterstock Images, 32, 102 (butterflyfish); Eric Carlander/Shutterstock Images, 33; Franco Banfi/NaturePL/Science Source, 36, 102 (manta ray); David Hall/Science Source, 38; Yann Hubert/Shutterstock Images, 40, 103 (reef shark); Tomas Kotouc/Shutterstock Images, 41; Aaron Bull/iStockphoto, 42; Sergey Uryadnikov/Shutterstock Images, 48; iStockphoto, 52, 53, 63, 71, 102 (sturgeon); James Pintar/Shutterstock Images, 54; Steve & Dave Maslowski/Science Source, 56, 102 (bass); Steve Howard/iStockphoto, 57; Dewald Kirsten/Shutterstock Images, 58; Chris K. Horne/Shutterstock Images, 62; Tom McHugh/Science Source, 64, 80, 81, 102 (hagfish), 102 (lungfish); Ron Newsome/US Navy, 66; Sakda Nokkaew/iStockphoto, 68; Nature and Science/Alamy, 72, 102 (lamprey); Book Worm/Alamy, 73; Nicolas Fernandez/Alamy, 74; Jody Ann/Shutterstock Images, 78; Eduardo Baena/iStockphoto, 79, 102 (salmon); Galina Savina/Shutterstock Images, 83; Jesus Cobaleda/Shutterstock Images, 84, 102 (stingray); Joe Quinn/Shutterstock Images, 85; Cigdem Sean Cooper/Shutterstock Images, 88; David Fleetham/Alamy, 89, 90, 103 (porcupinefish); Pete's Photography/iStockphoto, 93; Louise Murray/Science Source, 98; Uladzimir Navumenka/Shutterstock Images, 99

Editor: Arnold Ringstad
Series Designer: Sarah Taplin

Library of Congress Control Number: 2020949099

Publisher's Cataloging-in-Publication Data

Names: Krekelberg, Alyssa, author.
Title: Essential fish / by Alyssa Krekelberg
Description: Minneapolis, Minnesota : Abdo Publishing, 2022 | Series: Essential animals | Includes online resources and index.
Identifiers: ISBN 9781532195525 (lib. bdg.) | ISBN 9781098215903 (ebook)
Subjects: LCSH: Fishes--Juvenile literature. | Fishes--Behavior--Juvenile literature. | Animals--Identification--Juvenile literature. | Zoology--Juvenile literature.
Classification: DDC 597.0--dc23

CONTENTS

INTRODUCTION 4

ALLIGATOR GAR 12

BLUE TANG 16

CHANNEL CATFISH 20

CLEARNOSE SKATE 24

ELECTRIC EEL 28

FOUREYE BUTTERFLYFISH 32

GIANT MANTA RAY 36

GRAY REEF SHARK 40

GREAT BARRACUDA 44

GREAT WHITE SHARK 48

LAKE STURGEON 52

LARGEMOUTH BASS 56

MANDARIN FISH 60

PACIFIC HAGFISH 64

SIAMESE FIGHTING FISH 68

SILVER LAMPREY 72

SOCKEYE SALMON 76

SOUTH AMERICAN LUNGFISH 80

SOUTHERN STINGRAY 84

SPOT-FIN PORCUPINEFISH 88

WHALE SHARK 92

YELLOWFIN TUNA 96

ESSENTIAL FACTS	100	SOURCE NOTES	108
FISH AROUND THE WORLD	102	INDEX	110
GLOSSARY	104	ABOUT THE AUTHOR	112
ADDITIONAL RESOURCES	106	ABOUT THE CONSULTANT	112

INTRODUCTION

There are more than two dozen species of anemonefish, also known as clown fish.

Fish have been swimming in Earth's oceans, rivers, lakes, streams, and ponds for more than 500 million years.[1] There are approximately 34,000 known species of fish, and each fish has its own distinct characteristics and behaviors.[2] Some fish have scales, while others have slimy skin. Most fish rely on their gills to breathe underwater, but there are certain fish that can breathe air. Some fish give birth to live offspring, and other fish lay egg cases. Fish can be aggressive and solitary, or they can be social and form schools.

Fish have served as an important human food source for millennia. Fossil records show that approximately 1.95 million years ago, the ancestors of modern humans ate fish.[3] Fish contain essential nutrients such as vitamin D and protein, along with important fatty acids that help people's brains and bodies function and grow. Scientists suggest that because of these health benefits and the overall consumption of more meat, our human ancestors were able to fuel their brain development.

INTRODUCTION

People also have a history of keeping fish as pets and as food sources. By approximately 2500 BCE, the Sumerians, who lived in present-day southern Iraq, had fish in artificial ponds. In 1000 BCE, Chinese people were raising carp to eat, and scientists think they were likely breeding fish for show. In fact, their selectively bred goldfish spread to Japan in the early 1500s CE, where they were purchased by nobility. In both China and Japan, goldfish were symbols of good luck, fortune, and wealth. Today people keep many fish species as pets in home aquariums.

Although humans have studied fish for centuries, scientists are still learning about these animals, and they continue to discover new species. The ocean is the largest habitat in the world, and researchers haven't fully explored its depths. Many mysteries remain about the creatures living in the ocean's diverse and deep environments, but scientists have a good grasp on the various categories that fish fall into.

FISH CATEGORIES

Scientists classify life in a series of increasingly specific groups. From broadest to narrowest, these groups are domain, kingdom, phylum, class, order, family, genus, and species. There are also intermediate levels, such as superclass and megaclass. Some types of animals are contained in a single class. For example, the class Mammalia contains all mammals. Fish are found in the superclass Agnatha, megaclass Chondrichthyes, and megaclass Osteichthyes.

INTRODUCTION

Agnatha are jawless fish that include hagfish and lamprey species. These fish lack scales and have slimy skin, eel-like or cylindrical bodies, and circular mouths. Agnatha are known as primitive fish because they've been around for a long time. There are about 100 known species alive today.[4] Chondrichthyes have skeletons that are made mostly of cartilage. There are about 1,000 known species in this group, including various kinds of sharks, rays, and skates.[5] Osteichthyes, or bony fish, are the largest category of fish. There are around 27,000 known species.[6] The lake sturgeon and the yellowfin tuna are two types of bony fish.

FUN FACT
Agnatha are the earliest type of fish found in the fossil record, dating back 500 million years.[7]

Every species has a unique scientific name. These names help people clearly distinguish different animals. Typically, everyday people use a species's common name when discussing it. But many fish have multiple common names. For example, the channel catfish is also known as the spotted catfish, the Great Lakes catfish, the chucklehead cat, and the northern catfish. But the fish only has one scientific name: *Ictalurus punctatus*. If someone uses a species's scientific name, then it's very clear what animal he or she is referring to.

FISH BODIES

All fish live in water and are vertebrates, meaning that they have backbones or similar structures. Most of them chiefly use their gills to breathe, have scales that serve as

INTRODUCTION

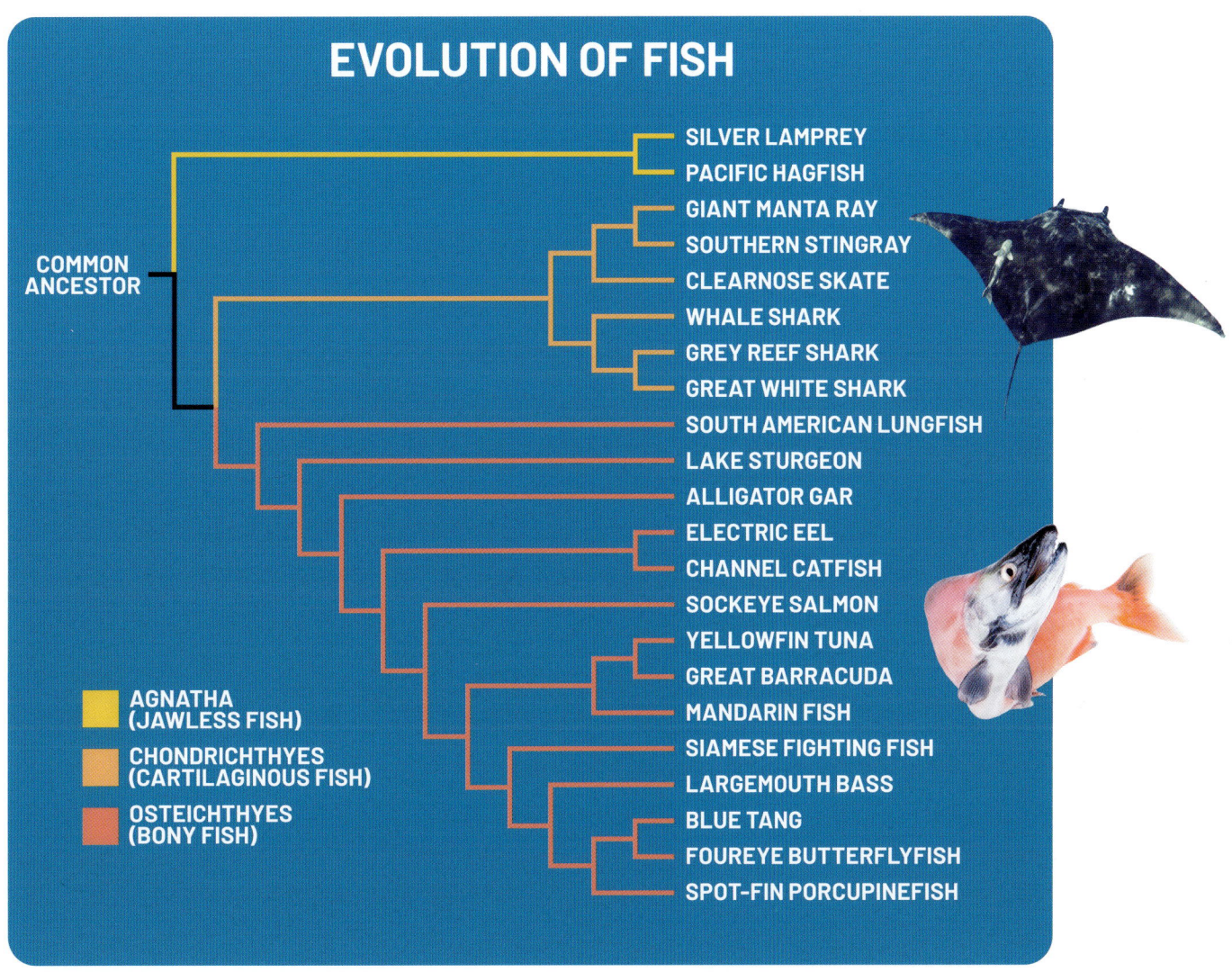

Fish adapted to have different features and behaviors that helped them survive in their environments. As new fish evolved, they outcompeted less efficient fish and drove them to extinction. Many surviving fish continued to adapt to new habitats, leading to the great diversity seen in fish species today. This graphic, a type of diagram known as a cladogram, sketches out the evolutionary relationships between the fish featured in this book.

protection, and are ectothermic, or cold-blooded. Ectothermic fish regulate their body temperatures using their surroundings, rather than using their own bodies to regulate temperature.

To move around, fish use different types of fins. These fins can be divided into two categories: median fins and paired fins. The median fins are found along a fish's centerline. They include the dorsal fin, which is on a fish's back and helps the fish navigate, protect itself, and stay upright. Median fins also include the anal fin and caudal fin. The anal fin is located toward the back of a fish's body, and it is used for stabilization. The caudal fin is also known as a tail fin, and it helps the fish propel itself through the water.

Paired fins are found on the left and right sides of a fish. They include pectoral fins, which are close to the head and help the fish turn and stay in place. They also include pelvic fins, which are on the lower right and left sides of the fish. Some fish have them near the front of their bodies, and some have them toward the back. These fins help stabilize the fish's body and also help it to stop. Given how different the bodies of fish can be, not all fish have every type of fin, and the fins do not always serve the same purpose.

Most bony fish have swim bladders that help them control their depth. The swim bladders of some primitive fish have evolved into lungs, and cartilaginous fish do not have swim bladders at all. Low-density oil in their livers helps make them more buoyant, but to maintain their depth, cartilaginous fish need to constantly swim.

INTRODUCTION

Some cartilaginous fish have many ampullae of Lorenzini. These organs help sharks, rays, and skates find prey. Animals produce weak electric fields when they move in the water. The ampullae pick up on these electric fields and tell cartilaginous fish where their next meals may be.

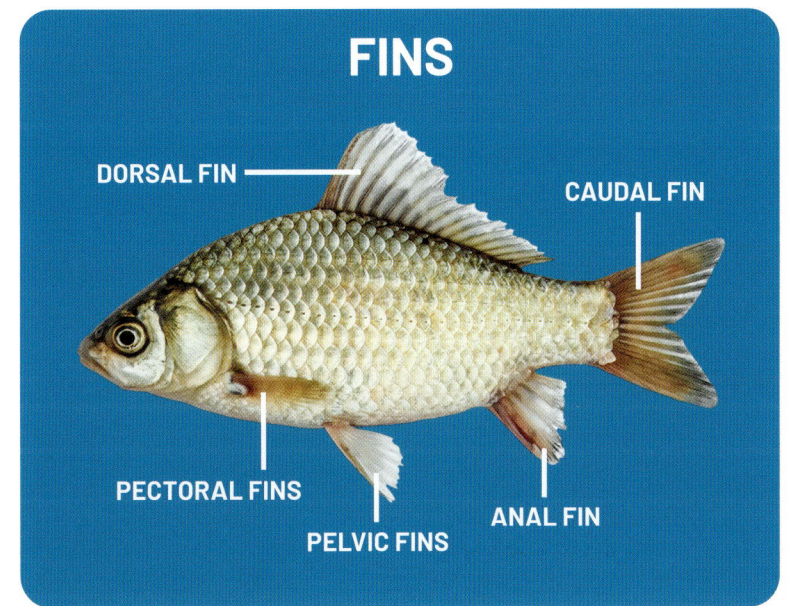

To navigate in both clear and murky waters, as well as shallow and deep waters, fish use their lateral line systems. These are sense organs that help fish move around. In most fish, one line runs down each side and branching lines stretch across the head. The lateral line systems perceive vibrations and movements in the water. They help fish recognize when objects and animals are close by.

IMPORTANCE OF THE ENVIRONMENT

Water covers 70 percent of Earth and offers a wide variety of habitats for fish.[8] Fish live in kelp forests, coral reefs, streams, rivers, ponds, lakes, the deep ocean, rushing rapids,

INTRODUCTION

pools of water in the desert, intertidal zones, and more. Without healthy habitats, fish populations suffer.

Human activities can harm fish habitats. Pollution, such as nutrient runoff caused by fertilizers and pet waste, can decrease oxygen levels in water or create harmful algae blooms. When too many algae grow at once, they have a toxic effect on aquatic life. Pollution not only hurts fish but also damages or destroys coral—an important habitat for many fish species.

Climate change plays a large role in habitat destruction. Earth is experiencing rising temperatures. Water expands as it gets warmer, and this, along with the melting of ice sheets and glaciers, makes the sea level swell. Climate change could wipe out important onshore wetlands that fish call home. In addition, the ocean is becoming more acidic due to climate change. This can kill coral reefs and harm fish's food supplies.

Dams and other human structures can drastically change ecosystems and even threaten the survival of species.

10

INTRODUCTION

More direct human activities disrupt fish populations too. Large dams and other water barriers stop fish from accessing hundreds of thousands of miles of streams and rivers, affecting their migration patterns. Millions of fish travel to their native habitats every year to spawn. However, many of them encounter human-made barriers that prevent them from reaching their spawning areas. This means they can't reproduce as effectively to sustain their population numbers.

ESSENTIAL FISH

This book highlights 22 remarkable fish species found in oceans, rivers, lakes, and streams. These fish encompass species from the Agnatha, Chondrichthyes, and Osteichthyes groupings, including the eel-like Pacific hagfish that slithers across the muddy ocean floor, the great white shark that rules the ocean as the biggest predatory fish, and the beautiful blue tang that darts in between colorful coral. The species are presented alphabetically by their common names. Each entry begins with a story showing the fish in its natural habitat, and the rest of the section is packed with fascinating facts and the latest scientific findings. A fact box provides key information about the species, and stunning photos bring these incredible creatures to life.

FISH EXTREMES

Fish are diverse animals that range in size and shape. One of the smallest is the dwarf minnow, which lives in the swamps of Southeast Asia and is 0.31 to 0.47 inches (8 to 12 mm) long.[9] The fish has a small, streamlined body and can fit on the tip of a person's finger.

The largest fish is the whale shark, which lives in warm ocean waters across the globe. It can reach 39 feet (12 m) in length and can weigh 15 tons (14 metric tons).[10] This shark has a flat, broad head, a large mouth, and a spotted body.

ALLIGATOR GAR

The alligator gar has a distinctive, alligator-like snout.

An alligator gar pushes its 6.5-foot (2 m) body toward the river's surface. It rests in the slow-moving water for a long time. Viewed from below, the fish looks like a harmless log. The alligator gar waits until a smaller fish slowly drifts by, unaware that it's getting closer and closer to a hungry predator. The gar waits for the perfect opportunity to strike, and then it lunges toward the fish with a surprising burst of speed. It pierces the fish with its long, fang-like teeth and bites down. Then the alligator gar swims away to consume its meal.

APPEARANCE AND DISTRIBUTION

There are seven gar species, and the alligator gar is the largest. In fact, it is one of the biggest freshwater fish found in North America. This gar isn't related to the alligator, but it gets its name from its alligator-like appearance. The gar has a long, slim body that's covered with hard, armor-like scales. The fish has brown to grayish-green coloring on its back, which fades to a yellow or white coloring on its stomach. Rows of teeth are set inside its broad snout.

The alligator gar has a modified swim bladder. This organ allows the fish to suck in air at the surface of the water, which helps the gar live in water with low levels of oxygen. In fact, an alligator gar is able to get 70 percent of its oxygen from the surface.[11]

ALLIGATOR GAR

The various gar species used to have a wider range than seen today. People have uncovered gar fossils in Europe, Asia, North America, and Central America. Today, gars only live in the Americas, with five gar species residing in the United States. Alligator gars live in the lower sections of the Ohio River, and their range extends south to the Gulf of Mexico. These fish have been spotted in Alabama, Arkansas, Florida, Georgia, Oklahoma, Tennessee, and Texas. Alligator gars also live in Nicaragua.

Some researchers believe alligator gars once lived farther north and that their range may have stretched all the way into Iowa. They think the fish may have lived in Kansas and Nebraska too. The gar's range is narrowing due to human activities, such as overfishing. Human-made structures to help control flooding, such as dams and dikes, may also have played a role in shrinking the alligator gar's breeding areas.

FUN FACT

Alligator gar eggs are toxic to people if consumed. The poison also deters other would-be predators, such as crustaceans.

REPRODUCTION AND DEVELOPMENT

There are still many mysteries about alligator gar reproduction. Scientists believe the fish reproduce in the spring, with April, May, and June as the primary spawning months in the southern United States. Scientists suspect the fish gather in large numbers to externally fertilize eggs. One or possibly multiple males swim next to a single female. Then the male fish release sperm and the female fish release eggs. The bright red eggs have an adhesive layer that allows them to stick to objects in the water. Females can reproduce at around 11 years of age, while males can reproduce when they're around six years old.

When alligator gars hatch, they look like small sticks. Yolk sacs are attached to the young gars, and they use the sacs as a food source. At this point in their lives, the gars have an adhesive spot underneath their snouts. They use this to stick to objects, such as rocks, and they rest in the water until they have finished consuming their yolk sacs. Large fish will prey on the young gars, but once the gars grow to three feet (1 m) long, the only predators strong enough to take them on are American alligators and humans.

ALLIGATOR GAR
Atractosteus spatula

SIZE
Up to 10 feet (3 m)

WEIGHT
Up to 350 pounds (160 kg)

RANGE
Southeastern United States, eastern Mexico, Nicaragua

HABITAT
Large, slow-moving fresh and brackish waters such as bays, rivers, reservoirs, bayous, oxbow lakes

DIET
Fish, blue crabs, small mammals, carrion, turtles

LIFE SPAN
26 years on average for males; 50 years on average for females

BLUE TANG

Blue tangs use their small mouths and teeth to feed on algae.

A group of blue tangs swims over a colorful coral reef in the Caribbean Sea. A few dart down to the coral and begin eating algae that grow there. The fish have sharp, tiny teeth that are well suited to scraping off algae, which make up the majority of their diet. By eating the algae, blue tangs can control algae populations and make sure the coral stay healthy.

Suddenly, the blue tangs scatter as a tiger grouper bullets toward them. The predator was hiding in the coral, waiting for prey to swim by. The grouper opens its mouth wide and sucks up a blue tang. Before it can deliver a killing bite, the blue tang extends the sharp spines that rest near its tail. The blue tang begins thrashing around, trying to slash the tiger grouper with its spines. Eventually, the blue tang gets free and swims into a crevice in the coral. It hides until the tiger grouper moves away.

STUNNING COLORS

A blue tang's body is flat like a pancake, and the fish has a pointed snout. Its dorsal fin runs from the front of its body all the way to its tail. The most remarkable feature of a blue tang, however, is its coloring.

Throughout its lifetime, a blue tang will go through three distinct color phases. A juvenile blue tang is bright yellow. When it gets a little older it develops gray stripes, and its yellow coloring changes into an orangish brown or blue. An adult is blue and sometimes purple, and it can have a yellow tail fin. An adult

FUN FACT

The fish Dory from the *Finding Nemo* movies is a regal blue tang (*Paracanthurus hepatus*). It is different from the blue tang (*Acanthurus coeruleus*).

blue tang can change colors for a period of time too. Sometimes, these fish have pale-white or near-black coloring.

REPRODUCTION AND BEHAVIOR

A blue tang changes colors when it is ready to mate. Its front half will become pale blue, and its back half will turn dark blue. Blue tangs gather in clusters of fewer than 20 fish. They meet around sandy patches of seafloor to mate, often in water that is 20 to 33 feet (6 to 10 m) deep with a current.[12]

The cluster of blue tangs will rush toward the surface, and the fish will release their eggs and sperm. Scientists call this behavior a spawning rush. The current takes the tiny fertilized eggs and pushes them out to sea.

Scientists think mating conditions depend on a

Juvenile blue tangs are yellow in color and often hide among coral reefs.

number of factors. The largest mating sessions seem to take place in the late afternoon, between three and eight days after a full moon during winter. Currents, the number of predators in the area, and light levels could also be factors.

Blue tangs move around a lot during the day but hide in the reef at night to stay safe from predators. A juvenile blue tang is small, lives alone, and often hides. As it gets bigger, the blue tang will expand its territory and protect the area from other fish.

Adult blue tangs are known for having three social styles. One style is territorial. A blue tang will chase other members of the same species away, and a fish that exhibits this behavior tends to swim slower and eat more than a blue tang exhibiting a different social style. Another style is wandering. A blue tang that wanders isn't typically aggressive and doesn't associate with other fish. It swims quickly, eats only a little, and is chased by fellow blue tangs and other fish species. The last social style is schooling, where blue tangs form a group, swim quickly, don't show aggressive behaviors, and eat at a rate between those of the fish in the other two styles.

BLUE TANG
Acanthurus coeruleus

SIZE
12 inches (30.5 cm) long

WEIGHT
1.6 pounds (0.72 kg)

RANGE
Western Atlantic Ocean, from New York to Brazil; around Ascension Island in the eastern Atlantic Ocean

HABITAT
Coral reefs and rocky or grassy areas in depths of 6 to 131 feet (1.8–40 m)

DIET
Algae

LIFE SPAN
12–15 years in the wild

CHANNEL CATFISH

The channel catfish is among the catfish species commonly fished and eaten by humans.

A male channel catfish approaches a weedy area in a lake. He finds the well-hidden nest that he and his mating partner created. The male catfish starts fanning the ground with his body and fins to clean the area. Above his eyes, his head is swollen, which is a signal that he is ready to mate.

The female channel catfish comes near the nest, and the male wraps his tail around her head. The female does the same to him. The male catfish shivers, causing the female to release a bundle of eggs that falls into the nest. He sprays the eggs with his sperm and then begins to chase the female, driving her away from the nest so she doesn't eat the eggs. The male swims near the eggs to guard them. The female keeps her distance from the nest, but she still protects her eggs by attacking any predators that come near. The small eggs hatch within four to ten days.

After hatching, the young catfish stay in the nest for approximately a week. The parents provide them with food. The male burrows into the mud near the nest and moves around to stir up tiny bits of food.

A FRESHWATER FISH

Channel catfish live in various bodies of fresh water, such as lakes and rivers. These fish are one of the most widespread species of catfish in North America, though they are found elsewhere around the world as well. A channel catfish has a long body, a forked tail fin, and an upper jaw that sticks out. It also has an extra dorsal fin made of connective tissue.

CHANNEL CATFISH

This fish does not have scales. Its dorsal side ranges from olive to pale gray, and its belly is yellow or whitish.

The channel catfish has eight whisker-like organs called barbels surrounding its mouth. These barbels have taste buds, which help the catfish find prey. The catfish's body also has taste buds that help the fish navigate through muddy, dark water. The channel catfish hunts actively when the water temperature is warm, between 50 and 94 degrees Fahrenheit (10–34°C), and it will eat mostly small fish, mollusks, and insect larvae.

> **FUN FACT**
> The heaviest channel catfish ever documented was caught in 1964 in South Carolina. It weighed 58 pounds (26 kg).[13]

To defend against predators such as the flathead catfish and the chestnut lamprey, the channel catfish has sharp spines on its pectoral and dorsal fins. It will straighten these spines when it is alarmed and try to stab the predator. In addition to being sharp, the spines are coated in mucus. If a catfish slashes a predator, the mucus can leave the predator with an infection.

CATFISH AND PEOPLE

The channel catfish is a popular sport fish. Anglers in North America use minnows, worms, and even chicken livers as bait. The catfish is most active at night, and many people fish either from the shore or on a boat after dark.

In some areas, fishers will noodle to find and seize this catfish. Noodling is when a fisher wades in shallow water and searches for a crevice or hole that a catfish may be hiding in. After finding a spot and obstructing potential escape routes, a fisher will put his hand into the hole and use his fingers to bait the fish into latching onto him. The fish's teeth are not sharp; noodlers say they feel like rough sandpaper. Once the fish latches on, the fisher can grab onto the catfish's mouth and pull it to the surface.

Farmers also raise channel catfish for consumption. This is a multimillion-dollar industry. Catfish is a popular food in the southern United States, and many farm-raised catfish are found in Alabama, Arkansas, Louisiana, and Mississippi.

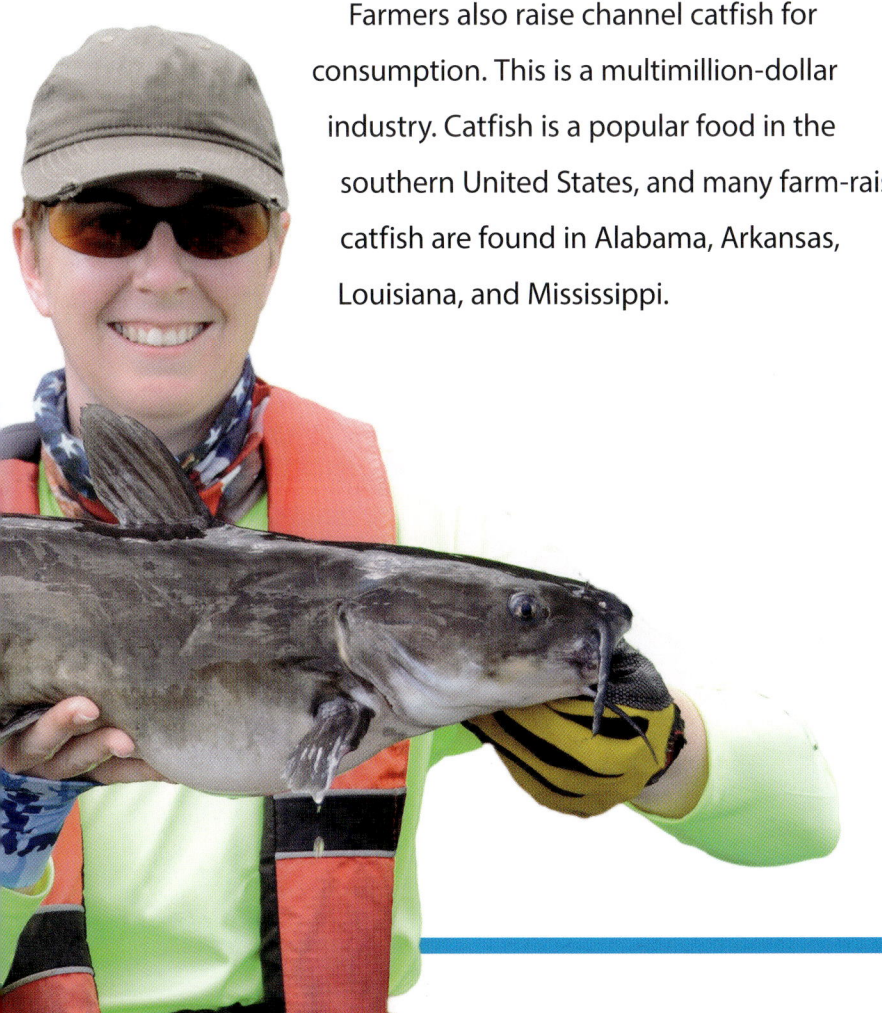

CHANNEL CATFISH
Ictalurus punctatus

SIZE
1.25–2 feet (0.38–0.60 m) long

WEIGHT
30 pounds (13.7 kg)

RANGE
Southern Canada, midwestern United States, Cyprus, Czech Republic, Malaysia, Romania, Slovakia, Spain

HABITAT
Creeks, lakes, ponds, reservoirs, rivers, streams

DIET
Freshwater invertebrates, small fish, sometimes vegetation

LIFE SPAN
14 years in the wild

CLEARNOSE SKATE

The coloring of the clearnose skate camouflages it against the seafloor.

A clearnose skate moves across the soft, sandy ocean floor by flapping its wing-like pectoral fins. After a while, the fish lies still on the sand. It has light-brown coloring with dark bars and spots on its back, and it blends in well with its environment.

The skate begins hunting, looking for crabs or shrimp to eat. Its movements are different from before. Instead of flapping its pectoral fins, the skate uses its pelvic fins to push itself across the sand—almost as if it is walking. The rest of its body stays relatively still, which prevents the water around it from moving too much. This helps the clearnose skate sneak up on its prey, which includes crabs, mollusks, and shrimp.

A SMALL SKATE

Compared to other skates, the diamond-shaped clearnose skate is rather small, with the largest being recorded at 2.8 feet (0.84 m) long. The clearnose skate is named for the two translucent sections of its snout. The rest of its dorsal side often ranges from brown to gray, and it has dark markings. Its underside doesn't have markings and can be cream or white.

Like all skates, the clearnose skate has a flat body. It also has thorns on its back that run from its tail to its shoulders. Adults display between 33 and 39 thorns, and juveniles can have 14 to 19.[14] In addition, a clearnose skate has small thorns on its shoulders.

Clearnose skates are usually seen in the Atlantic Ocean, from waters along Massachusetts to southern Florida. These skates also reside in the eastern Gulf of Mexico. The clearnose skate lives in warm waters generally ranging from 41 to 81 degrees Fahrenheit (5–27°C). The skate will migrate to stay within its preferred temperature range. In the summer and early fall, it will live offshore in the northern part of its range. In the winter and spring, it can be found near the shore in the southern part of its range. This skate lives on sandy ocean bottoms and in rocky areas.

REPRODUCTION

Water temperatures influence when a clearnose skate will breed, as it prefers water at 61 to 72 degrees Fahrenheit (16–22°C) during this time. Males reach sexual maturity between the ages of two and four, and females can reproduce starting between four and six years old.

FUN FACT

Skates, sharks, and rays have an unusual ability to resist diseases. Due to this, researchers have used clearnose skates to study cancer.

When clearnose skates reproduce, the male comes toward the female from behind. He latches on to one of her pectoral fins with his teeth and curves his tail so it is below hers. The skates will sometimes hold this position for one to four hours before they begin to breed. The skates start breeding when the male puts a structure called a clasper into the female's reproductive region. The male's sperm goes into the female, where it can be stored for approximately three months.

After the female's eggs are fertilized, she will deliver them in the ocean. To do this, the female arches her back and shakes her pelvic area to release an egg capsule, a protective structure that encloses her eggs. Her shaking helps to partially submerge the capsule into the ocean sand. She will lay a second egg capsule minutes or hours later.

Water temperature plays a role in whether the eggs will develop. They won't develop in water that is warmer than 75.2 degrees Fahrenheit (24°C). With the right water conditions, it can take approximately three months for the eggs to hatch. The baby clearnose skates are small—approximately five to six inches (12.7–15.2 cm) long.[15] They are completely independent after hatching and do not receive assistance from their parents.

The egg capsule of a clearnose skate

CLEARNOSE SKATE
Raja eglanteria

SIZE
Up to 2.8 feet (0.84 m) long

WEIGHT
Up to 7.7 pounds (3.5 kg)

RANGE
Western Atlantic Ocean from Massachusetts to Florida; eastern Gulf of Mexico

HABITAT
Bays and estuaries at depths of 328–1,083 feet (100–330 m)

DIET
Crabs, mollusks, shrimp, small fish

LIFE SPAN
5 years or more in the wild

ELECTRIC EEL

Electric eels live in shallow waters.

An electric eel's snake-like body moves smoothly through the murky river water. The eel doesn't have good eyesight, so it uses a weak electric field to navigate. This helps the eel sense nearby objects, such as prey.

The eel moves toward a group of fish, sensing their movements and heartbeats. It lets out two quick pulses of electricity that shock the fish, making them twitch and showing the eel exactly where they are in the water. Then the eel releases a stronger electric pulse, which paralyzes the fish. The eel opens its mouth wide and swallows a fish whole.

Later, a caiman—an animal that is related to alligators—approaches the eel as it swims in shallow water. It snatches for the eel with its large, powerful jaws. The eel jumps from the water and presses its body against the caiman. It delivers a series of powerful pulses to shock the predator. Soon the caiman is lying stunned, temporarily unable to move. The eel slips away into the muddy water.

ELECTROCUTING AND BREATHING

The electric eel can reach up to 8.2 feet (2.5 m) in length, and its serpentine body can range in color from brownish black to gray. It has a long anal fin that allows it to dart forward and backward or even to hover in the water. The electric eel has a big mouth and a somewhat flat head. Some of the most remarkable features of an electric eel are found inside its body: the electric organs.

FUN FACT
The electric eel isn't actually a member of the eel family—it's a type of knife fish. It got its name from its eel-like body.

An electric eel has three organs that produce electricity. These are known as the main organ, the Hunter's organ, and the Sachs' organ. These organs take up approximately 80 percent of the eel's body, and the rest of its vital organs are crammed into its front.[16] The main organ and most of the Hunter's organ create the most powerful electric pulses, which are meant to immobilize the eel's prey and scare off predators. The rest of the Hunter's organ as well as the whole Sachs' organ give off less powerful pulses. These help the eel navigate through dirty waters and communicate with potential mates. The eel has thick skin covered in slime to help protect itself from its own electricity.

When electrocuting large prey, the eel relies on a certain tactic. It wraps its body around the prey in order to increase the strength of its electric field. Then, the eel will send out multiple quick shocks, exhausting the other animal's muscles until it can't fight back.

The eel's ability to produce electric shocks isn't the only remarkable thing about the fish. Although the electric eel has gills, that's not the primary way it breathes. The water the eel lives in doesn't have much oxygen, so the eel gets approximately 80 percent of its oxygen by inhaling air.[17] It goes to the surface once every ten minutes or so to suck up air through its mouth. The eel's mouth has pink folds in it that absorb oxygen.

REARING YOUNG

The dry season is when electric eels reproduce. The male creates a nest with his saliva, and then the female lays her eggs in it. During this season, females can lay approximately 1,200 to 1,700 eggs.[18]

Males will protect the eggs until the rainy season comes. Scientists think this behavior occurs because during the dry season there is increased competition for food, and more predators may try to consume the eggs. When the electric eel larvae come out, they will devour any eggs that have not yet hatched. As they grow larger, they'll change their diet to fish. This is when the male leaves his young to survive on their own.

ELECTRIC EEL
Electrophorus electricus

SIZE
6–8 feet (1.8–2.4 m) long

WEIGHT
44 pounds (20 kg)

RANGE
Northeastern South America, including the lower and middle Amazon River basin

HABITAT
Shaded, muddy river bottoms and swamps

DIET
Small fish

LIFE SPAN
15 years in the wild

FOUREYE BUTTERFLYFISH

The large, eye-like spot on the foureye butterflyfish may help confuse or intimidate predators.

A foureye butterflyfish darts through light-colored coral in the Gulf of Mexico's tropical waters. Its small, flat, disc-shaped body helps it move comfortably through gaps in the coral. To get through some spaces, the fish swims upside down or sideways. Every once in a while the fish pauses to eat. It uses its small mouth and short snout to nip at tiny invertebrates resting in the coral's crevices, and the fish also uses its bristle-like teeth to scrape food off the coral.

The foureye butterflyfish has a light-gray body with a yellow tint and black, V-shaped bars. Near its tail fin is a large, black circle surrounded in white that looks like an eye. These false eyes are found on either side of the fish's body. Its real eyes have black vertical stripes over them to help hide them from predators.

As the butterflyfish swims around, a moray eel spots it. The eel's long, ribbon-like body is nestled in the coral, with only its head poking out. The eel's small eyes lock onto the butterflyfish as it gets closer. It stares at the fish's false eyes, and it strikes in that direction.

The eel reaches for the fish with its wide mouth. Other fish might dart forward. But the foureye butterflyfish seems to swim backward and away from the predator. The fish quickly moves into a small space within the coral so the eel can't attack again. The butterflyfish's false eyes have saved it from becoming a meal for the moray eel.

A LONG-LASTING BOND

When a foureye butterflyfish gets to be 3.5 inches (9 cm) long, it is able to reproduce. Unlike many other fish species, the foureye butterflyfish picks one mate to form a long-lasting bond with. The fish will pair up early in their lives, and if the two fish ever lose sight of one another, one will dart toward the surface to scan the area for its partner.

When it's time to mate—a process that usually takes place between February and May—the foureye butterflyfish pair undergoes a long, lively ritual. The two fish start by circling one another. Eventually one of them will swim away quickly, forcing the other to follow, and they will playfully chase after one another until dusk.

Once dusk falls, the female butterflyfish releases 3,000 to 4,000 eggs into the sea and the male sprays his sperm at them.[19] The eggs float among the plankton in the water. They hatch within 24 hours after being fertilized. The larvae are distinctive, with their heads surrounded by bony plates and armor that eventually become scales. The larvae's silvery-gray coloring makes them semitransparent and helps them hide from predators.

At its juvenile stage, a foureye butterflyfish begins to develop its adult coloring. The black line appears across its eye, the false eye begins to emerge on its back end, and its scales begin to take on gray-and-yellow coloring. The most noticeable

FUN FACT

Researchers think a large female foureye butterflyfish can produce 100,000 to 200,000 eggs each year.[20]

FOUREYE BUTTERFLYFISH
Chaetodon capistratus

SIZE
Up to 5.9 inches (15 cm) long

WEIGHT
0.06–0.13 ounces (1.6–3.7 g)

RANGE
Western Atlantic Ocean, from Massachusetts to Brazil

HABITAT
Coral reefs and other inshore areas at depths of 6–65 feet (1.8–19.8 m)

DIET
Tiny marine invertebrates

LIFE SPAN
7 years maximum in the wild

difference between a juvenile and an adult butterflyfish is that the juvenile does not have thin, black, V-shaped lines on its body. Instead, the juvenile has one large black bar on its front end. In addition, there is dark coloring around its false eyes.

GIANT MANTA RAY

The giant manta ray is the largest species of ray on Earth.

A giant manta ray flaps its large pectoral fins to glide through the warm water off the coast of northern Peru. From the tip of one pectoral fin to the other, the ray is approximately 22 feet (6.7 m) wide. As it moves, the manta ray looks like it's flying underwater.

The ray swims with its large, rectangular mouth open. It has two fleshy flaps in front of its mouth known as cephalic lobes, which curl into an O shape to help the fish direct food toward its mouth. As it moves, the ray catches tiny plankton floating in the ocean water. Inside the ray's mouth are gill rakers. They filter out water through the ray's gills but redirect the plankton for the fish to eat.

Nearby, more than a dozen other giant manta rays are feeding on the plankton-rich waters too. They weave around each other. Some giant manta rays stay so close to the surface that their backs skim the waves above. Other rays swim a little deeper, scattering schools of fish in their paths.

THE MASSIVE MANTA

> **FUN FACT**
> Manta rays will sometimes somersault while eating in order to get more plankton into their mouths.

Giant manta rays are the largest rays, and they live throughout the world's tropical, subtropical, and temperate ocean waters. They can be found around the southern coast of Africa, along the southern reaches of California to northern Peru, in the Gulf of Mexico, and from North Carolina to southern Brazil. The rays are often found at the ocean's surface and usually don't swim deeper than 394 feet (120 m).[21] People often see giant manta rays close to shore, where the water is warm and plankton thrive, but these fish have been known to swim farther out to sea as well.

A giant manta ray's back can range in color from grayish blue to black, and it has a white underbody with gray specks. These specks are arranged differently on every manta ray. Researchers can use them to identify individual rays.

The biggest manta ray scientists have studied had a wingspan of almost 30 feet (9.1 m). Typically, females are larger than males, with female wingspans ranging between 18 and 22 feet (5.5 and 6.8 m) and males reaching 17 to 20 feet (5.2–6.1 m).[22] Despite their large size, manta rays aren't dangerous to people. Their only predators are large sharks and humans.

GRACEFULLY SWIMMING

The giant manta ray is a solitary fish that is not territorial. It can start reproducing when it is approximately five years old. A ray will search for a mate between early December and throughout April. Mating happens in warm waters that range between 78 and 84 degrees Fahrenheit (26–29°C) and in depths of 33 to 66 feet (10–20 m). During this time, manta rays are sometimes observed jumping completely out of the water to potentially attract a mate.

Giant manta rays have symbiotic relationships with a few fish species. When parasites and dead skin accumulate on a ray's body, wrasse fish flock to the ray and begin snatching off these things—effectively cleaning the ray. Remora fish also benefit from giant manta rays. They attach to a manta and ride along with it. The fish will feast on the ray's parasites and will also capture plankton as the ray swims.

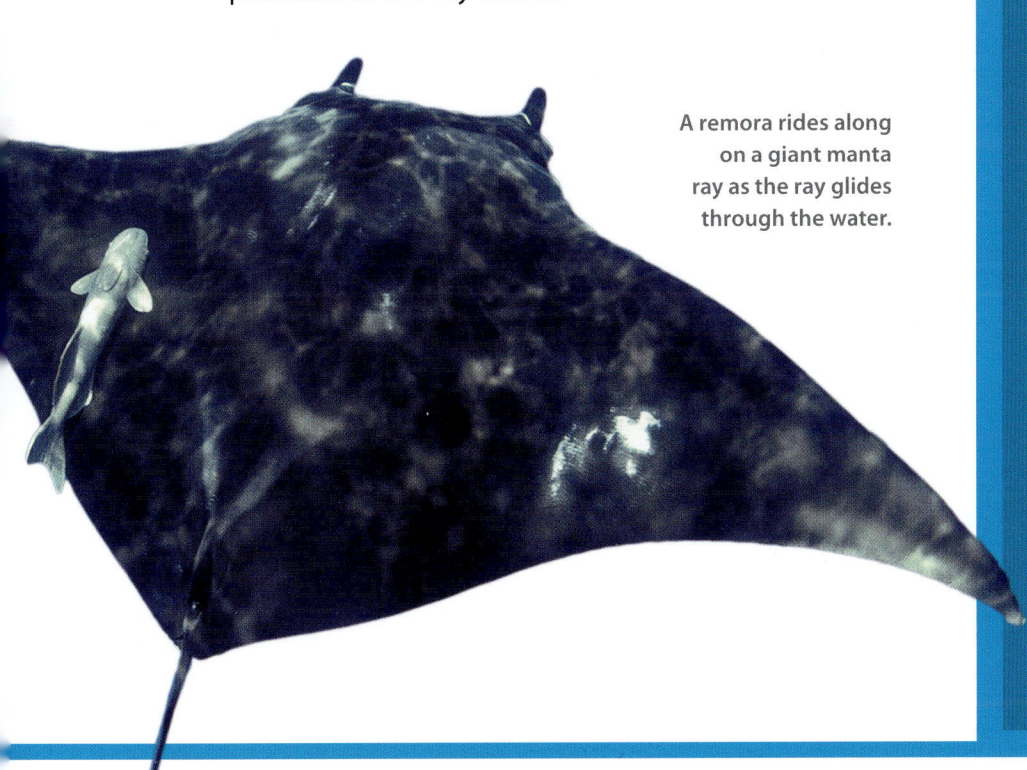

A remora rides along on a giant manta ray as the ray glides through the water.

GIANT MANTA RAY
Manta birostris

SIZE
Wingspan 17–22 feet (5.2–6.8 m)

WEIGHT
Up to 1.5 tons (1.4 metric tons)

RANGE
Tropical, subtropical, temperate oceans worldwide

HABITAT
Near shore, from surface to depths of 394 feet (120 m)

DIET
Plankton

LIFE SPAN
About 40 years in the wild

GRAY REEF SHARK

Gray reef sharks have light undersides and darker dorsal sides, helping camouflage them in the water.

During the day, a school of approximately 30 gray reef sharks swims lazily through the water in the Indian Ocean. The sharks stick close to the ocean's bottom, near a coral reef drop-off, and wait for night. As the water darkens, the gray reef sharks begin swimming faster around the coral.

Long, slim needlefish also circle the coral. Suddenly, a gray reef shark makes a dash at one of them, and the needlefish darts away. The shark chases it and gets a bite, filling the water around it with dark blood. The needlefish escapes, but a handful of other gray reef sharks are close behind, swimming in what appears to be a pack.

Each shark is looking out only for itself. One shark is able to securely grasp the fish's head in its sharp, serrated teeth before swimming away into the darkness to devour its prey.

APPEARANCE AND BEHAVIOR

The gray reef shark has big eyes and a long, round snout. The shark has two dorsal fins on its back. The first one is located above the pectoral fins, and the second is close to the anal and tail fins.

The shark's back can range in color from bronze to dark gray, and its belly is white. The gray reef shark is sometimes mistaken for other, similar-looking shark species, such as the blacktip reef shark. Both sharks have dark coloring along the edges of their tail fins. But the gray reef shark lacks the blacktip's distinctive black-tipped dorsal fin. In certain gray reef shark populations, such as those in the Red Sea and in the western Indian Ocean, the shark's first dorsal fin has a white edge.

Gray reef sharks are territorial, and they sometimes display a certain aggressive behavior toward other sharks and even people who are diving near them. A gray reef shark will move its pectoral fins downward, arch its back, and sway its head from side to side while swimming to show that it is unhappy that another shark or a diver is nearby. If the shark or diver doesn't leave, the gray reef shark may get more aggressive.

A gray reef shark is able to reproduce at approximately seven years old. A sexually mature female will give off chemical signs showing she's prepared to mate. When a male recognizes this, he will chase after the female and aggressively bite her with his sharp teeth. Then, he will insert his claspers, which are between

FUN FACT

Gray reef sharks play an important role in the coral reef ecosystem as the top predators. They keep the fish population numbers at a healthy level.

his pelvic fins, into the female to fertilize her eggs. The female holds her fertilized eggs for approximately a year before giving birth to between one and six live babies.

NEAR-THREATENED SPECIES

The International Union for Conservation of Nature (IUCN) is an international organization that keeps track of animal conservation issues throughout the world. It lets people know if species are in danger of extinction. In 2020, the IUCN said gray reef sharks were endangered.

Gray reef sharks are dependent on coral reefs. With climate change affecting reefs, the sharks' habitat is in danger of diminishing drastically as coral die. In addition, these sharks are in danger due to overfishing. This is because the sharks are found close to shore, and they often gather in a single, predictable location, making the sharks easy for fishers to snare. These factors, combined with the slow sexual maturation and small litter sizes of gray reef sharks, may be driving down the population of this species.

GRAY REEF SHARK
Carcharhinus amblyrhynchos

SIZE
4–8.4 feet (1.2–2.6 m) long

WEIGHT
41 pounds (18.5 kg) on average

RANGE
Indian and Pacific Oceans

HABITAT
Tropical and subtropical waters near coral reefs and drop-offs, at depths of 0–164 feet (0–50 m)

DIET
Fish, squid, octopuses, shrimp, lobsters

LIFE SPAN
25 years maximum in the wild

GREAT BARRACUDA

There are more than 20 species of barracuda, and the great barracuda is among the largest.

A great barracuda pushes its long, tube-shaped body through the ocean water with a powerful sweep of its tail. It swims near the edge of a reef and searches for its next meal. The barracuda catches sight of a humpback red snapper and barrels toward it. It snatches the snapper into its strong jaws and slices into the fish. The barracuda has sharp, blade-like teeth that make it a dangerous predator. Its upper teeth slip into spaces in the lower jaw, and the barracuda is able to completely close its mouth while holding onto the snapper, cutting it in half. The barracuda consumes one half of the fish, and then it swallows the second half.

A while later, the barracuda begins herding a school of fish. It swims back and forth, ushering the fish into shallower water. The barracuda isn't particularly hungry, but it keeps the fish in line so they can't escape. Another predatory fish swims by and tries to attack the fish in the school, but the barracuda strikes first and scares the single fish away. The barracuda protects the school of fish until it gets hungry. Then it turns to feast on them.

AN OCEAN PREDATOR

Great barracudas live in tropical and subtropical ocean waters, and they are most often seen in the western Atlantic between Massachusetts and Brazil, including in the Caribbean Sea and Gulf of Mexico. Great barracudas are also

FUN FACT

A great barracuda has some teeth that point backward. These teeth stop squirming fish from escaping a barracuda's powerful grip.

seen in the Indo-Pacific region, the Red Sea, and areas of the eastern Atlantic. They are rarely observed in the eastern Pacific. A great barracuda prefers to live near the shore in seagrasses, mangroves, and coral reefs. While the barracuda often lives close to the water's surface, the fish has been spotted at depths of up to 325 feet (99 m) as well.[23]

The great barracuda has a pointed snout and a lower jaw that projects outward. Coloring on its back can be bluish gray or brown, and individuals may have from 18 to 23 dark-colored bars in this area. The fish's sides have a green sheen that fades to silver, along with dark spots. Its stomach is white.

People have observed barracudas as long as 6.5 feet (2 m). Using their thin, long bodies, barracudas can swim up to 36 miles per hour (58 kmh), making them effective at ambushing and catching their prey.[24] Due to their size and quickness, adult great barracudas hardly have any natural predators. However, sometimes predators such as tuna, sharks, and goliath groupers attack small adult barracudas. A juvenile great barracuda will live in areas that shield it from predators, such as in seagrasses and mangroves, until it is approximately two years old. By that time, the juvenile has grown large enough to leave the shallow water to live around the reefs.

GREAT BARRACUDAS AND HUMANS

Great barracudas are curious, and they will follow swimmers and divers in the water. They are enticed by shiny things that they associate with fish, and barracudas have been known to strike at people displaying watches, jewelry, or diving knives.

If a great barracuda attacks, it often takes only one quick bite out of a person. Such a bite, however, can cause a significant injury. One documented attack in 1960 happened when a person got bitten twice by a great barracuda and had to get 31 stitches. However, it's rare that great barracudas attack people without provocation, and experts note that attacks can easily be prevented if people are mindful of what they're wearing or holding so as not to entice a barracuda.

GREAT BARRACUDA
Sphyraena barracuda

SIZE
6 feet (1.8 m) long

WEIGHT
83 pounds (37.6 kg)

RANGE
Most tropical and subtropical oceans worldwide; rarely in the eastern Pacific Ocean

HABITAT
Close to shore in seagrasses, mangroves, coral reefs; in the open oceans

DIET
Fish

LIFE SPAN
14 years in the wild

GREAT WHITE SHARK

Great white sharks may jump into the air when attacking their prey.

Off the coast of South Africa, a colony of Cape fur seals rides the choppy, blue waves to the open ocean to find fish. Beneath the water, a great white shark patrols an area the seals must pass through. The shark spots the swift, dark shapes and launches its massive body toward them.

Using the element of surprise, the shark breaches the water's surface directly below a seal. The great white opens its mouth wide, revealing large, triangular, serrated teeth that are ideal for ripping apart prey. The seal falls right into its jaws, and the shark bites down.

The shark breached the water's surface at approximately 40 miles per hour (64 kmh).[25] This speed allows the shark to leave the water completely. With the seal gripped securely in its mouth, the great white shark flips in the air, revealing its white underside, and falls headfirst into the water, where it consumes its catch.

THE LARGEST PREDATORY FISH

The great white shark is the largest predatory fish in the ocean, its body reaching up to 23 feet (7 m) in length. Females are often larger than males. A great white shark has a large dorsal fin, and the coloring on the shark's back ranges from light to dark gray. It has a long, powerful tail and a narrow, slightly pointed snout that can smell blood in the water from 3 miles (4.8 km) away.[26]

Great whites are typically solitary creatures. They keep their personal space when approaching or swimming beside another shark, but they'll actively discourage other great whites from targeting the same prey as them. If two great whites are looking to consume the same prey, the sharks will raise their tail fins and hit the water's surface to push water toward the other shark. They will also dramatically beat their tails in a single direction and roll on their sides. Sometimes, one shark will simply block another shark with its body so the other shark can't reach the prey.

SHARK ATTACKS

In 2020, people reported 57 unprovoked shark attacks globally. These attacks ended up killing ten people.[27] It's sometimes difficult for

> **FUN FACT**
> Orcas will work together to take down a single great white shark. They are after the shark's liver—a high-fat organ that can weigh up to 600 pounds (272 kg).[28]

UNPROVOKED SHARK ATTACKS IN 2020

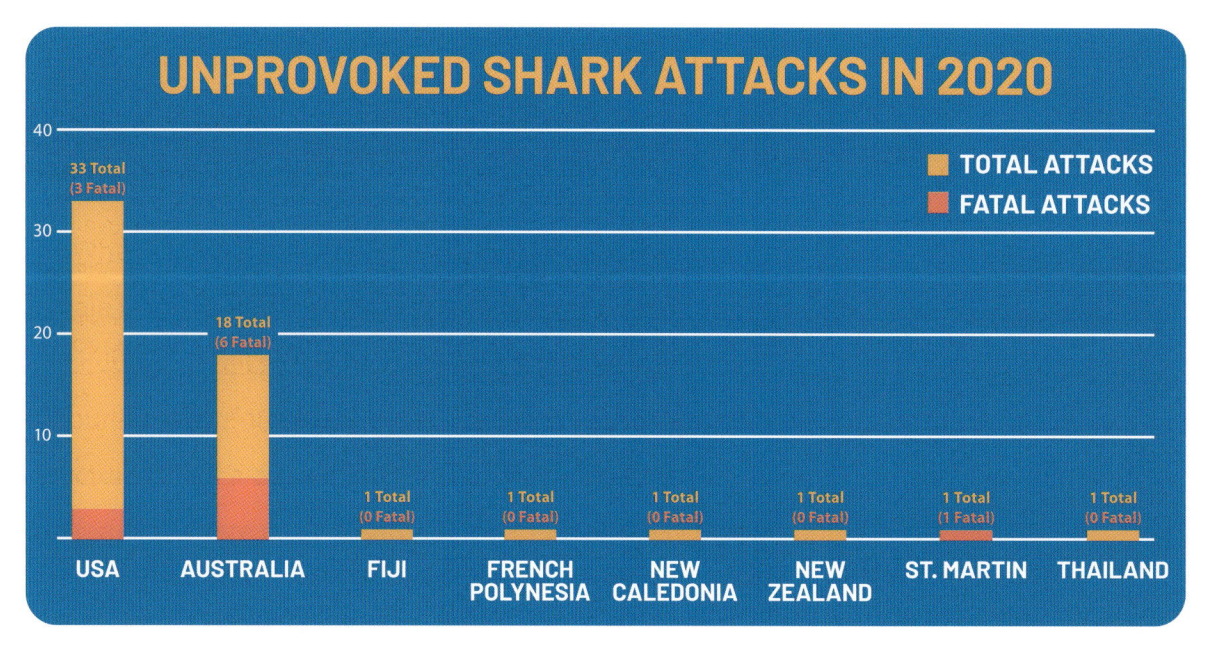

Country	Total Attacks	Fatal Attacks
USA	33	3
Australia	18	6
Fiji	1	0
French Polynesia	1	0
New Caledonia	1	0
New Zealand	1	0
St. Martin	1	1
Thailand	1	0

Great white sharks, tiger sharks, and bull sharks are the three most common sharks that attack people. Most shark attacks occur when people are surfing or doing other water board sports.

people to identify what shark species was involved in the attack, but scientists know that great white sharks are one of the five most dangerous sharks to people. This could be in part because of how close humans get to great whites. People swim or surf in areas where great white sharks are located, bringing them in close contact with the creatures.

Great white sharks don't actively hunt people. They're curious animals and will investigate foreign objects—such as people and surfboards—by taking exploratory bites. A. Peter Klimley works at the University of California, Davis, and is an expert in marine animal behavior. He says that sharks "bite a lot of things that don't resemble any of their known prey. They don't tear these things to pieces. They take a bite, feel them over, then move on."[29] However, even exploratory bites can hurt a person. In 2009, Hannah Mighall was attacked by a great white shark when she was surfing. Ten years after the attack, her leg still had the scars from the shark's teeth and was weaker than her other leg.

GREAT WHITE SHARK
Carcharodon carcharias

SIZE
13–23 feet (4–7 m) long

WEIGHT
2.5 tons (2.3 metric tons)

RANGE
Temperate ocean waters worldwide; also in tropical and cold waters

HABITAT
Open oceans and near the coasts, from the surface to depths of more than 4,265 feet (1,300 m)

DIET
Marine mammals, fish

LIFE SPAN
70 years in the wild

LAKE STURGEON

The lake sturgeon lives in dark environments, so it relies on senses other than sight to navigate.

Below the blue waves in Lake Erie, a 6.5-foot (2 m) lake sturgeon swims through the dimly lit fresh water. It coasts over slimy rocks and green weeds, then dips closer to the bottom of the lake, looking for food. The fish doesn't have good eyesight, so it uses its barbels to touch the muddy bottom.

A barbel sweeps over something that's more than just mud. The sturgeon quickly opens its mouth, sucks up a snail that was resting on the lake floor, and then continues to look for more food. The sturgeon's prey—which also includes crayfish, insect larvae, worms, and small fish—are tiny when compared with how massive the lake sturgeon is, so most of the sturgeon's day is dedicated to feeding.

LIVING IN LAKES

The lake sturgeon lives in temperate waters in North America. It is found in the northern sections of the continent, such as in the Great Lakes, Mississippi River, and Hudson Bay. The fish lives close to the bottoms of lakes or rivers—preferably ones that have gravel or sand.

    A lake sturgeon can reach up to 9 feet (2.7 m) in length. The fish has a snout that projects outward, four barbels near the mouth, and thick lips that it uses for sucking up prey. The sturgeon has gray-green colors and bony plates, which are hard and act like a shield. By the time the lake sturgeon reaches adulthood, the only predators that threaten this fish are humans and occasionally lampreys.

The plates on a lake sturgeon look different depending on how old it is. When it is young, a sturgeon's plates have hooked spines, protecting it from predators such as herons. When the sturgeon gets older, its plates take on a smooth appearance. In addition, as a sturgeon ages its snout becomes less pointy.

CONSERVATION EFFORTS

In the 1800s and early 1900s, people began hunting lake sturgeon in large numbers. At first, sturgeon were targeted by fishers because they were seen as a nuisance. When looking

FUN FACT

The sturgeon family was around when dinosaurs roamed Earth. Conservationist Jeff Miller notes, "They've survived relatively unchanged for 200 million years."[30]

for other fish, people would sometimes accidentally catch sturgeon, and the fish would damage their fishing gear. Then the food industry found out about the sturgeon and wanted to turn the fish's unfertilized eggs into caviar. Between 1879 and 1900, the fishing industry on the Great Lakes caught approximately four million pounds (1.8 million kg) of sturgeon each year.[31] This overfishing, in addition to the construction of human-made dams that harmed the sturgeon's ability to spawn, greatly decreased the sturgeon population.

Conservationists are trying to save this threatened species. Some state organizations, such as the New York State Department of Environmental Conservation, capture male and female lake sturgeon, take their sperm and eggs, and fertilize the eggs. The organizations bring the eggs to a hatchery, where the eggs hatch into baby sturgeon. Experts take care of them until they grow large enough to be released back into their native habitats. Conservationists hope their work will help lake sturgeon population numbers bounce back.

LAKE STURGEON
Acipenser fulvescens

SIZE
9 feet (2.7 m) long

WEIGHT
198 pounds (90 kg) on average

RANGE
North American fresh water including the Great Lakes, Mississippi River, Hudson Bay

HABITAT
Bottoms of lakes or rivers, ideally with gravel or sand

DIET
Worms, snails, small fish, crayfish, insect larvae

LIFE SPAN:
55 years on average for males in the wild; 80–150 years for females in the wild

LARGEMOUTH BASS

The largemouth bass is a native fish of North America and is the state fish of both Georgia and Mississippi.

The summer sun beats down on the lake below, heating the water. It's nearly warm enough for the male largemouth bass to start preparing to spawn. He swims around the lake, searching for a spot to make a nest. The bass finds an area in shallow water where the bottom is pebbly, and he begins making a little depression in the pebbles where the eggs will go.

Once the water reaches 59 degrees Fahrenheit (15°C), the male largemouth bass searches for a mate. He finds a female swimming in deep water and ushers her to his nest. Once she's near it, he begins circling her so she doesn't swim away and starts gently running into her—a sign that she should drop her eggs. The female is of average size, so she releases approximately 4,000 eggs into the nest.[32] Bigger females are able to lay more eggs. The male immediately sprays his sperm on the eggs to fertilize them.

The female largemouth bass swims away, but the male stays at the nest. He protects the eggs from predators and fans away any silt that may fall on the eggs. He does this for three to seven days until the eggs hatch. The baby bass are tiny at 0.12 inches (3 mm) long, and the male continues to protect them for a few more days.

When the baby bass reach approximately 1 inch (2.5 cm) in length, they leave the nest and the male is free to go. At this point, the male largemouth bass is hungry—he hasn't eaten since he started protecting the eggs. He begins hunting and will eat any food he finds, including his own young.

INHABITING FRESH WATER

Largemouth bass live all across the United States. Fishers can find them in the Great Lakes, the Saint Lawrence River, Hudson Bay, the Mississippi River basin, and Atlantic Ocean drainage areas ranging from North Carolina to

LARGEMOUTH BASS

FUN FACT

Over time, the largemouth bass spread from the eastern United States to the rest of the world because of its popularity as a sporting fish.

Florida and even northern Mexico. The bass prefer to live in areas with clear water and lots of vegetation, and they can be found in lakes, creeks, rivers, ponds, and swamps.

At night, the largemouth bass will find shelter in deep water, such as under a log. Once morning comes, the fish will relax under lily pads or in other shaded areas, or it will swim above vegetation at a shallow depth. In the evening, the bass begins to search for food. Bass use vegetation for cover while hunting for prey.

Young largemouth bass are preyed upon by yellow perch, walleye, muskies, northern pike, and some waterbirds. Adults, however, are often the top predators in many areas and are attacked only by bald eagles and humans. This has to do with how fast they can swim and the protections their bodies offer.

Largemouth bass have thick, long, olive-green bodies, and some bass have a stripe that runs along their sides. They have two dorsal fins, and the front one has nine to 11 spines that help protect the fish from becoming prey.[33] This bass gets its name from its large mouth, which stretches past its eyes.

LARGEMOUTH BASS
Micropterus salmoides

SIZE
1.5 feet (0.45 m) long

WEIGHT
3.3 pounds (1.5 kg)

RANGE
Originally from the eastern United States but has been introduced in Europe, Guam, Japan, Lebanon, New Zealand, the Philippines, South Africa, throughout the United States

HABITAT
Warm waters in ponds, lakes, swamps, creeks, reservoirs, big rivers

DIET
Insects, small fish, worms, mice, turtles

LIFE SPAN
6 years maximum for males in the wild; 9 years maximum for females in the wild

MANDARIN FISH

The mandarin fish is instantly recognizable for its striking colors and patterns.

As night falls on the western Pacific Ocean, a group of colorful mandarin fish gathers on a coral reef. There are more males than females, and the males need to compete for attention. A male mandarin fish points his dorsal fin upward to impress the females and to intimidate the males. The spine on his dorsal fin is so long that, if bent backward, it would almost reach his tail.

He catches the eye of a female, and she moves closer to him. She's smaller than the male, and she leans against his pectoral fin as they swim upward a few feet away from the reef. The way the two fish move together and how their pectoral fins beat vigorously against the water make it almost look like the pair is dancing. Suddenly, the two fish drop back toward the coral, leaving behind a white cloud of sperm and eggs that they've released at the same time. The eggs and sperm mingle together in the moving water, and the current moves the now fertilized eggs back toward the reef, where they will hatch within the next 12 hours.

EXTRAORDINARY COLORS

A mandarin fish is easily recognizable by its body shape and stunning colors. The fish can grow to 2.8 inches (7 cm) long, has a puckered mouth, and has a wide head with eyes that are positioned outward. Instead of scales, the fish has smooth skin that is covered in mucus, which smells awful and tastes bitter. Its skin also has cells that create a poison to protect the fish from predators. Mandarin fish have colorful bodies with blue, turquoise, orange, and yellow stripes.

A mandarin fish needs warm water to survive. It lives in the western Pacific Ocean, which includes areas near Hong Kong, Australia, Indonesia, New Guinea, and the Philippines. The fish often swims around shallow lagoons and coral reefs. The mandarin fish is a picky eater, and it depends on the reef for food. The fish's outward-facing eyes help it find food in the dimly lit environment.

FUN FACT
Some experts think the mandarin fish's bright coloring is a warning to predators that the fish is poisonous.

The mandarin fish is known for its shy nature. During the day, the fish will often stay still and hide. When it does move, the fish has a distinctive way of perching and hopping across coral reef branches. To move, the fish has to flick its pectoral fins quickly—almost like a hummingbird does with its wings in order to fly.

AQUARIUMS

Due to its beautiful coloring, many people seek out the mandarin fish to add to their home aquariums. This is a big trade in the western Pacific. In fact, some local economies in Hong Kong and the Philippines earn a large chunk of money from the aquarium trade.

However, the mandarin fish is difficult to care for. It needs a relatively large tank that allows for at least 30 to 75 gallons (114–284 L) of water.[34] Also, the mandarin fish is a picky eater, often eating only tiny crustaceans called copepods. If a fish hobbyist doesn't have the proper food in a tank, the mandarin fish will starve to death. In addition, a male will attack another male of the same species if they are in the same tank. The combination of these things leads to a drastically decreased life expectancy for pet mandarin fish. In the wild, the fish can live between ten and 15 years. In captivity, the mandarin fish typically lives for only two to four years.

MANDARIN FISH
Synchiropus splendidus

SIZE
2.8 inches (7 cm) maximum

WEIGHT
Unavailable

RANGE
Western Pacific Ocean

HABITAT
Shallow lagoons and coral reefs

DIET
Small crustaceans

LIFE SPAN
10–15 years in the wild; 2–4 years in captivity

PACIFIC HAGFISH

Pacific hagfish sometimes curl up on the ocean floor.

A Pacific hagfish weaves around the muddy ocean floor. It has a long, eel-like body and uses its paddle-like tail to slither through the water. The hagfish's eyes are small, so it uses its sensitive barbels to touch its surroundings and its single nostril to detect prey.

A dead fish sinks in the cold water nearby, and the hagfish picks up its scent. The hagfish twists through green seaweed until it finds the pale fish lying still on the ocean floor, and the hagfish clasps on with its teeth. The hagfish has a jawless, ring-shaped mouth with a couple of rows of sharp teeth, and it uses these to burrow into the fish. Then the hagfish pulls and tears the dead fish apart using two sets of tooth-like structures on its tongue.

Other Pacific hagfish join in on the feast. They shred flesh from the fish and tunnel their heads inside of it. Their serpentine bodies stick out from the carcass and squirm in the water. The hagfish release mucus from small holes on the sides of their bodies, which keeps other would-be predators away from their meal. When the hagfish are done, only the dead fish's bones and skin are left behind.

THE OCEAN ECOSYSTEM

The Pacific hagfish is essential to its ecosystem. It consumes dying or dead creatures that would otherwise clog up the ocean, and it recycles nutrients to keep its habitat healthy. The hagfish is often found at depths of between 131 and 328 feet (40–100 m) in cold, Pacific Ocean waters, but it has also been found at extreme depths of up to 2,077 feet (633 m).[35]

FUN FACT
The Pacific hagfish has a slow metabolism and can go up to seven months without consuming anything.

A Pacific hagfish has scaleless skin that is typically either tan, gray, or brown on its dorsal side. Since it doesn't have scales to protect itself from predators, such as harbor seals, it creates mucus. When the mucus hits the water, it makes a thick slime that gets into the mouth or gills of a predator and can sometimes smother it. The hagfish's unusual body has another defense mechanism. Since the hagfish's skeleton is made of

PACIFIC HAGFISH

A scientist demonstrates the stickiness of the thick slime given off by the Pacific hagfish.

cartilage, the fish is able to tie itself into and out of a knot and twist away from predators. Scientists think a hagfish also uses this behavior to clean slime off its body.

A PRIMITIVE FISH

Throughout the past 300 million years, hagfish have remained relatively unchanged. Scientists know this because of the fossil record, which tells them something important about the hagfish's evolution. Tom Munroe works at the Smithsonian National Museum of Natural History as a fish zoologist. He notes, "It's an indication, not that they've stalemated and are not evolving, but that they have arrived at a body plan that is still very successful today."[36]

Although scientists have learned about the evolutionary history of the Pacific hagfish, the fish's reproductive behavior is still a bit of a mystery. Researchers know that females lay 20 to 30 eggs during each cycle at depths of 49 to 82 feet (15–25 m).[37] When the eggs hatch, they look like miniature versions of adult hagfish and are fully independent.

PACIFIC HAGFISH
Eptatretus stoutii

SIZE
1–2 feet (0.3–0.6 m) long

WEIGHT
1.8–3 pounds (0.8–1.4 kg)

RANGE
North and South Pacific Ocean

HABITAT
Cold waters in depths of 131–328 feet (40–100 m); on muddy or rocky ocean bottoms

DIET
Dying or dead fish and mammals; likely marine invertebrates

LIFE SPAN
40 years maximum in the wild

SIAMESE FIGHTING FISH

Captive Siamese fighting fish are often bred to have vivid colors.

A male Siamese fighting fish, also known as a betta fish, drifts to the pond's still surface and draws in a sip of air. Mucus in his mouth covers the air bubble, and the fish spits it out and watches it float toward the water's surface. The male does this over and over again, spending hours creating this nest composed entirely of air bubbles. He takes a break for a bit to snatch a few insects that rest on the water's surface, but then he continues his work.

A female Siamese fighting fish comes toward the nest. Her fins are close to her body and she keeps her head down—a sign to the male that she's ready to release her eggs. The two fish start circling and gently hit one another on their sides. Then the male pushes the female over and wraps his body around her, strengthening his grip. He holds her like this for a bit, fertilizing her eggs, and then releases her.

At this point, the male drifts below the female as she stays upside down. The female starts laying between three to seven eggs. As the eggs sink toward the bottom of the pond, the male dashes for them and collects the eggs with his mouth. The mucus in his mouth coats them, and he places them in his nest. When the female stops laying eggs, the male embraces her again and fertilizes the next batch of eggs. The eggs are released and the process is repeated. The female may eventually lay several hundred eggs in all. As soon as she's done, the male chases her away and becomes the sole caretaker of the nest.

FUN FACT

If a female Siamese fighting fish is not interested in mating with a male, the male can become aggressive and will tear her fins and scales.

HABITAT AND BEHAVIOR

Siamese fighting fish live in slow-moving freshwater areas with low levels of oxygen and lots of vegetation. These areas can include rice paddies, streams, and ponds. To survive and thrive in low-oxygen waters, the Siamese fighting fish has what is known as a labyrinth organ. This organ lets it take in air through the mouth at the water's surface.

During the dry season, a Siamese fighting fish's habitat may dry up, but the fish has adapted to survive without a lot of water. The fish will submerge itself into the mud or clay at the bottom of its habitat and can live there until rain comes to end the dry spell. However, the mud or clay where the fish is buried needs to be somewhat moist for the fish to survive.

A Siamese fighting fish needs a stable temperature. This fish is native to Thailand, where a water temperature of 75 degrees Fahrenheit (24°C) is typical. If the fish lives in an area where the temperature is too high or too low, its metabolism can get disrupted. For instance, if the water gets above 81 degrees Fahrenheit (27°C), the fish's metabolism speeds up, making the fish use its energy too quickly. The high temperature can make the fish age faster than it normally would. On the other hand, if the temperature is below 70 degrees Fahrenheit (21°C), the fish's movements will slow down.[38]

The Siamese fighting fish is well-known for its tendency to attack fish of the same species. Males in particular are quite aggressive, and they will fight other males to maintain their territories. This behavior led people to capture and breed the fish to fight for sport.

CAPTIVE FISH

In the 1800s, people in Thailand began to breed this fish to fight competitively. In the wild, males can fight for only up to 15 minutes, but people wanted to extend this time.

Breeders began cultivating the fish to fight for more than one hour, and people bet on the outcomes. This activity is illegal in some places, including the United States.

All Siamese fighting fish have streamlined bodies, but their colors differ drastically depending on whether they're wild or captive fish. Due to captive breeding, fish used in aquariums are much more colorful and can be bright red, royal blue, lime green, and more. In addition, captive fish often have large, almost feathery-looking fins. In the wild, Siamese fighting fish usually have more muted colors.

Siamese fighting fish for sale at a market in Vietnam

SIAMESE FIGHTING FISH
Betta splendens

SIZE
2.9 inches (7.5 cm) long

WEIGHT
0.092 ounces (2.6 g) on average for males; 0.086 ounces (2.4 g) on average for females

RANGE
Native to Thailand; sold worldwide in pet stores

HABITAT
Slow-moving waters with thick vegetation

DIET
Insects, algae

LIFE SPAN
2 years on average in captivity

SILVER LAMPREY

A silver lamprey caught accidentally by sea lamprey fishers in the Great Lakes region

In the spring, the water temperature in Lake Superior slowly increases, signaling to the female silver lamprey that it is time to spawn. The lamprey is approximately eight inches (20 cm) long and shaped like an eel. She uses her long dorsal fin, which runs from the middle of her back down to her tail, to navigate in the clear water.

In the distance, the silver lamprey sees a large lake sturgeon and propels toward it. The lamprey has an O-shaped mouth with rows of sharp teeth, and she uses these to attach to the sturgeon. The sturgeon doesn't pay much attention to the lamprey and unwittingly gives the smaller fish a ride upstream toward the lamprey's ideal habitat to spawn: a clear, large river with a sandy and gravelly bottom.

The female lamprey detaches from the sturgeon and is soon approached by a male lamprey. The two begin building a nest made of gravel. The pair works for three days, and the end result is a nest that's approximately 4.3 inches (11 cm) deep and 11.8 inches (30 cm) wide.[39] Once it's finished, the female latches onto a rock with her mouth and the male grabs onto the female's head. They arrange their bodies close to one another, then at the same time release sperm and eggs. The fertilized eggs fall into the nest. Adult silver lampreys are capable of reproducing only once during their lives, and they will swim off to die after this process.

A PARASITIC FISH

Silver lampreys live in lakes and rivers—often in the Great Lakes area but also in the Hudson, Mississippi, Ohio, and Saint Lawrence rivers. Sometimes these fish can be seen in Kentucky waterways. Young lampreys live in streams and rivers, and adults occupy lakes.

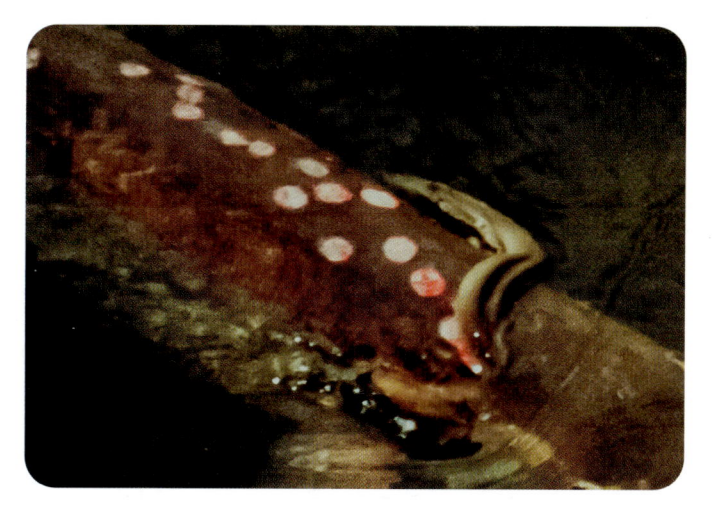

A lamprey leaves several disc-shaped markings on a muskellunge.

SILVER LAMPREY

Lampreys of all kinds use their circular mouths with sharp teeth to cling onto other fish.

Lampreys in the larval stage are mostly grayish brown or brown. They burrow into the bottoms of rivers, through sand and muck, and consume small particles such as algae and pollen. They do this for approximately four to seven years before becoming adults.

Young adult lampreys often have tan or slate coloring with lighter stomach colors. Once they're fully mature, the lampreys turn a blue-gray or gray color. Adults are parasitic. They fasten themselves to large fish, cut through the fish's skin, and then use their mouths to suck up the fish's body fluids and blood. A silver lamprey will rarely kill its host fish, but its sharp teeth often leave circular scars. Host fish for the lamprey include lake sturgeon, paddlefish, carp, northern pike, walleye, and more. Once in

FUN FACT
Fishers sometimes use both young and small adult silver lampreys as bait to catch catfish and bass.

its adult form, a silver lamprey will live for only another year or two before reproducing and then dying.

LAMPREYS AND THE ECOSYSTEM

Young silver lampreys help their ecosystems by recycling nutrients. When they eat things such as algae, pollen, and other small organic matter, they break down and recycle the nutrients. These nutrients can then be taken in by other animals living in the river.

Sometimes people mistake silver lampreys for sea lampreys. While the two fish look somewhat similar, they are different species with different effects on ecosystems. Silver lampreys are native to the Great Lakes region and beyond. While these lampreys feed on fish, they don't decimate fish populations like sea lampreys do. Sea lampreys are an invasive species in the Great Lakes. They originally lived only in the Atlantic Ocean, but human activities—such as establishing shipping routes—allowed sea lampreys to come into the Great Lakes and feed on fish there. Over the course of its life, a sea lamprey can kill 40 pounds (18 kg) of fish.[40] The species has caused some fish populations in the Great Lakes to collapse.

SILVER LAMPREY
Ichthyomyzon unicuspis

SIZE
4–13 inches (10–33 cm) long

WEIGHT
0.056–3.7 ounces (1.6–104 g)

RANGE
Fresh water in the northern United States, southern Canada

HABITAT
Large lakes and rivers with clear water

DIET
Young eat algae, pollen; adults eat fish

LIFE SPAN
5–9 years in the wild

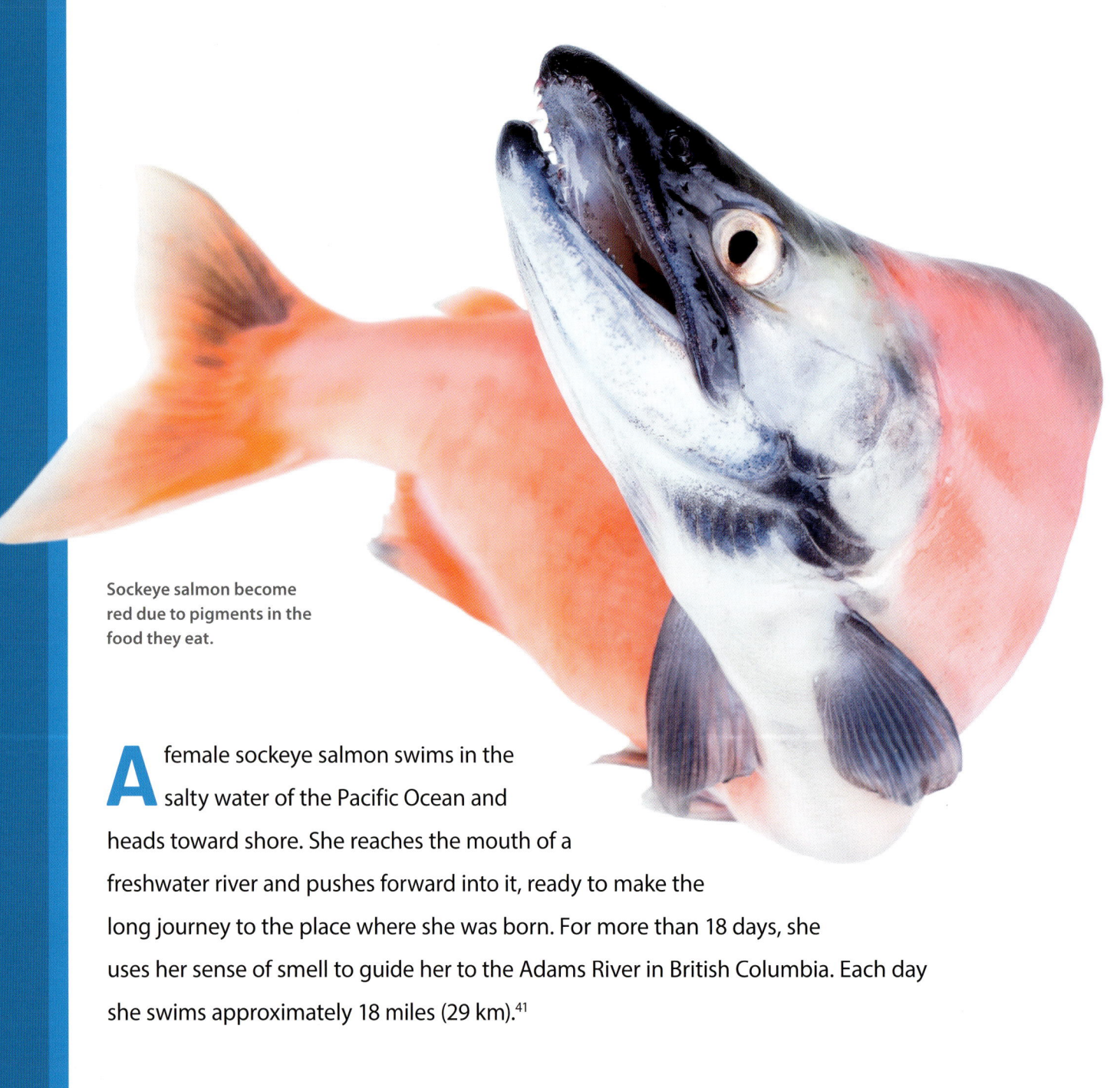

SOCKEYE SALMON

Sockeye salmon become red due to pigments in the food they eat.

A female sockeye salmon swims in the salty water of the Pacific Ocean and heads toward shore. She reaches the mouth of a freshwater river and pushes forward into it, ready to make the long journey to the place where she was born. For more than 18 days, she uses her sense of smell to guide her to the Adams River in British Columbia. Each day she swims approximately 18 miles (29 km).[41]

Other sockeye salmon join her on this journey. The fish have long, red bodies and green heads. Most males have hooked jaws and humped backs. The salmon weave through the cold river water and past slimy rocks. Suddenly, a grizzly bear lunges for one of the salmon and rips the fish apart with its sharp claws and teeth. The rest of the fish try to swim quickly through this part of the river, but not all of them are successful, because other bears are searching for their next meals in the area too.

Approximately one million sockeye salmon reach the Adams River. The females dig nests in the river's gravelly bottom and can each lay more than 4,000 eggs.[42] Some of the males come along and show themselves off to the females, hoping to be selected as mates. The females judge the males based on size and color. A male's large size is proof that he was able to get food in the ocean, and a vibrant red coloring shows that he is healthy. Once a female picks a mate, she allows him to fertilize her eggs, and she pushes gravel over her eggs. Then the pair leaves.

SURVIVING IN FRESH AND SALT WATERS

Sockeye salmon are born in freshwater rivers, streams, and lakes in North America. They stay in fresh water for one to three years before entering the Pacific Ocean. At this point, the salmon don't look much like their spawning parents. They have light stomachs, dark

FUN FACT

Out of the 4,000 eggs a female sockeye salmon can lay, on average only two of them will live to adulthood and spawn themselves.

SOCKEYE SALMON

backs, and an overall silvery color. Their kidneys and gills start changing to help them survive in salt water, and the fish avoid light, seeking deep water in which to swim.

Once they reach the Pacific Ocean, sockeye salmon eat mostly zooplankton and small fish. This diet allows them to grow and become strong. In the ocean, sockeye salmon are prey for lampreys, sharks, and other marine mammals such as seals. Salmon live in the ocean for approximately two or three years. At this point, they're fully mature and are ready to make their way back to the rivers where they were born so they can spawn.

GIVING BACK TO THE ECOSYSTEM

When sockeye salmon travel to spawn, they grow weak. The trip is long and arduous, and many salmon cease to eat once they hit fresh water. Once they spawn, the salmon don't have the energy to go back to the ocean, and they die.

When a sockeye salmon dies, its body releases nutrients back into the environment. These nutrients help feed the newly hatched salmon, as well as plants both in the water and on land.

SOCKEYE SALMON
Oncorhynchus nerka

SIZE
Up to 2.7 feet (0.83 m) long

WEIGHT
5–15 pounds (2.3–6.8 kg)

RANGE
Eastern Pacific Ocean, from Alaska to California; they spawn inland in North America

HABITAT
Born in fresh water but move to the ocean, where they live at depths of 49–108 feet (15–33 m)

DIET
Zooplankton, small fish

LIFE SPAN
4–5 years on average in the wild

SOUTH AMERICAN LUNGFISH

Unlike nearly all other fish, the South American lungfish does not breathe using gills.

The South American lungfish pushes its eel-shaped body through the swamp's calm water. It lifts its head to the surface and opens its mouth wide, sucking in the air above, before submerging itself again. This fish has lungs, and it needs to stay near the surface in order to breathe air.

During Brazil's dry season, temperatures can reach 90 degrees Fahrenheit (32°C), and low rainfall can cause some bodies of water to dry up. At a certain point, the lungfish finds itself slithering across a slick surface of mud after the swamp's water vanishes. Its mouth opens and shuts as it breathes. The lungfish begins to burrow into the mud to keep its body from getting dry, and the fish doesn't stop until it's approximately 1.6 feet (0.5 m) underground.[43] It surrounds itself with clay but keeps a few holes leading to the surface for air. Then the lungfish slows down its metabolism. It can survive like this for months, and the fish doesn't eat during this time. Instead, the lungfish uses up its body's fat reserves and muscle tissue to stay alive. Once the rainy season comes, the fish emerges from its low-energy state and wriggles back to the surface to swim in the water once again.

A FISH WITH LUNGS

The South American lungfish has a slender body that can reach approximately four feet (1.2 m) long. It also has stringy pelvic and pectoral fins that are often moving and touching objects to help the fish sense its surroundings. This ability is especially useful since the lungfish has poor eyesight. An adult lungfish has solid tooth plates rather than separate teeth, which help it crunch down on invertebrates.

Juvenile and adult lungfish have different colorings. A juvenile has bright yellow markings, while an adult is either gray or black. Another major difference between young and mature lungfish is in regard to their gills and lungs. The fish's lungs are modified from its swim bladder. When the South American lungfish is young, it has gills that help it breathe. When it reaches seven weeks old, its gills begin to disappear and the fish becomes more reliant on its lungs. At that point, the fish needs to start going to the surface to breathe.

FUN FACT
The South American lungfish will drown if it can't reach the surface to breathe.

HABITAT AND REPRODUCTION

South American lungfish are partial to stagnant waters without much of a current, such as those in lakes and swamps. They're found in South America—including in Venezuela, Peru, Paraguay, Colombia, French Guiana, Bolivia, Brazil, and Argentina—and their preferred temperature range is between 75 and 82 degrees Fahrenheit (24–28°C). The lungfish is often found in the Amazon River basin.

Scientist don't know much about how a South American lungfish reproduces. They know the fish breeds in the rainy season, which gives the adult more options for where it can build its nest underwater. They also know that a male and female work together to make a nest for their young, and when the eggs are fertilized the male protects them. In addition, a male will provide oxygen to its young to help them develop. During the breeding season, a male's pelvic fins turn into a feathery structure that gives off oxygen from his own blood and absorbs carbon dioxide.

SOUTH AMERICAN LUNGFISH
Lepidosiren paradoxa

SIZE
4 feet (1.2 m) long

WEIGHT
Unavailable

RANGE
South America

HABITAT
Stagnant fresh waters, such as lakes or swamps, from the surface to 1.6 feet (0.5 m) deep

DIET
Weeds, algae, bony fish, plants, invertebrates

LIFE SPAN
8 years on average in the wild

SOUTHERN STINGRAY

Like other types of rays, the southern stingray uses its wide, flat body to glide through the water as if flying.

In the shallow water off the coast of Florida, a southern stingray slowly glides above the ocean's bottom. The stingray's eyes rest on the top side of its body, so the fish uses its well-adapted sense of smell and its electroreceptors to search for prey. When it detects something in the sand, the stingray hovers over the area. Then it flaps its large pectoral fins on the ocean's bottom to uncover a small crustacean. The stingray scoops it up with its mouth, which rests on the bottom of its body. Nearby, a small fish follows the stingray and snatches the little pieces of food the stingray has kicked up while trying to get at the crustacean.

SOUTHERN STINGRAY

The stingray moves on and soon finds another creature to eat. This time, the stingray uses its mouth to blow out a jet of water, disturbing the sand and unveiling a clam. The stingray uses its flat teeth to crush the clam's shell and get to the soft flesh inside.

When daytime approaches, the southern stingray buries itself in the soft, tan sand. The sand helps it hide from predators such as the great hammerhead shark. Its gills—which are located on the bottom side of its body—are pressed against the sand. The stingray uses two holes on the top of its head, called spiracles, to breathe.

BODY AND HABITAT

The southern stingray has a diamond-shaped body, and females are larger than males. The stingray also has wide pectoral fins that, while in motion, give the illusion that the fish is flying in the water. The fish ranges in color from gray-green to olive brown on top; its bottom is white. It also has a tail that grows longer than the length of its body—sometimes almost twice as long. Along the tail is a sharp, venomous spine that the stingray uses to defend itself. Although the stingray is not an aggressive creature, it has been known to use its spine to protect itself when stepped on by humans. This situation can occur when the stingray is hiding under the sand in shallow waters and swimmers or divers come across it.

Southern stingrays live in warm areas, and people have seen them in waters ranging from 82 to 90 degrees Fahrenheit (28–32°C). They stick close to the shore at depths of around 6.6 feet (2 m).[44] Southern stingrays live in subtropical and tropical areas in the western Atlantic Ocean, including in the Gulf of Mexico, the Caribbean Sea, and as far south as Brazil.

FUN FACT
Female southern stingrays give birth approximately once a year. The female's size plays a role in how many offspring she will have; large females often have more.

STINGRAYS AND THE ENVIRONMENT

A southern stingray plays an important role in the ecosystem by serving as both predator and prey in the ocean food chain. In addition, the southern stingray has symbiotic relationships with Spanish hogfish and bluehead wrasses, which pick off mucus and parasites on the stingray, thus helping the stingray while feeding themselves.

The southern stingray also kicks up food for the double-crested cormorant. This bird dives into the ocean to catch fish, using its webbed feet to propel itself through the water.

When the stingray disturbs the ocean sand to find prey, it sometimes displaces fish. Double-crested cormorants have been known to dive and swim near the stingray to catch these fish in shallow water.

SOUTHERN STINGRAY
Dasyatis americana

SIZE
Wingspan 6.6 feet (2 m)

WEIGHT
Up to 214 pounds (97 kg)

RANGE
Subtropical and tropical waters in the western Atlantic Ocean, including in the Caribbean Sea, Gulf of Mexico, as far south as Brazil

HABITAT
Shallow waters near coasts, estuaries with silt or sandy bottoms

DIET
Worms, crustaceans, small fish

LIFE SPAN
12–13 years in the wild

SPOT-FIN PORCUPINEFISH

When not inflated, the spot-fin porcupinefish looks largely similar to other types of fish.

In the western Atlantic Ocean, a spot-fin porcupinefish cruises over an old shipwreck. The ship has been underwater for so long that colorful coral decorate its surface, and tropical fish use holes and gaps in the ship as their homes. The porcupinefish has a round body covered with spines that rest flat against the fish's body. The fish ducks into one of the ship's many crevices and swims around for a bit, looking for sea urchins, snails, or hermit crabs to eat.

The fish eventually leaves the shipwreck and heads out a little farther into the ocean. A dolphinfish catches sight of it and moves quickly to strike. Startled, the porcupinefish falls back on its best defense mechanism: it sucks in water and inflates its flexible skin to three times its normal size, making its spines stick outward. The fish also releases a poisonous toxin. Both of these things make the dolphinfish hesitate and then swim away to look for easier prey. Once the animal is gone, the porcupinefish deflates itself by blowing out the extra water it was holding.

INSHORE LIVING

The spot-fin porcupinefish's spines are adapted scales, and the fish is typically green or brown in color with dark markings speckling its body. The porcupinefish has big eyes above a strong jaw and fused teeth that are ideal for cracking open the hard exoskeletons of its food sources. The fish's rubbery lips serve as protection from those potentially sharp exoskeletons.

SPOT-FIN PORCUPINEFISH

These fish live in the Pacific, Atlantic, and Indian Oceans, as well as in the Mediterranean Sea and Red Sea. Adults typically like inshore areas at depths between 9.8 and 65.6 feet (3–20 m), and they are seen among caves, shipwrecks, lagoons, ocean

FUN FACT
Porcupinefish are passive, curious creatures that will sometimes swim near divers. Scientists consider this species to be relatively intelligent.

ledges, reefs, and seamounts. They live in crevices and holes and come out at night to hunt. Juveniles live in the open ocean and hide in seaweed until they're approximately 8 inches (20 cm) long, at which point they flock to shallow water and develop into adults.

An adult spot-fin porcupinefish is often alone, except for when it breeds. Scientists haven't been able to study the porcupinefish's mating habits, but they do know that their eggs are shaped like spheres and are swept into the ocean current. The eggs hatch approximately five days after they're fertilized. Larvae and juveniles live in the ocean's seaweed and are targeted by predators such as the dolphinfish and billfish.

Although scientists aren't sure how spot-fin porcupinefish mate, they can make some educated guesses by observing a very similar fish known as the balloonfish. Balloonfish mate when the water heats up to approximately 77 degrees Fahrenheit (25°C). At that time, a few males will escort a single female to the water's surface, triggering her to release her eggs, and all of the males will spray their sperm. The process may be similar for the spot-fin porcupinefish.

SPOT-FIN PORCUPINEFISH
Diodon hystrix

SIZE
16 inches (40 cm) long on average

WEIGHT
6.2 pounds (2.8 kg)

RANGE
Tropical and subtropical waters worldwide

HABITAT
Crevices or holes near the shore at depths of 9.8–65.6 feet (3–20 m)

DIET
Sea urchins, snails, hermit crabs

LIFE SPAN
At least 10 years in captivity

WHALE SHARK

The whale shark is Earth's largest known fish species.

Near the ocean's surface, a whale shark glides through the blue water, pushing its massive body with a few graceful sweeps of its tail. The shark opens its large mouth and begins sucking in water filled with microscopic plankton. The plankton get stuck in the shark's mouth, and the water the shark drew in gets filtered out through its gills. The whale shark does this over and over again, getting most of the food it needs to support its 39-foot (12 m) body from the tiny organisms.

The whale shark is constantly on the move, following the plankton-rich waters. In February, the shark arrives off the coast of Venezuela, where other whale sharks swim around peacefully. Smaller fish are also there, and they gather together to traverse the warm water in schools. The shark dives deeper into the water and eyes the schooling fish near the surface. Then the shark moves upward, keeping its mouth open, and swims directly through the school. It captures a mouthful of the small fish and consumes them.

A GENTLE GIANT

The whale shark is the largest fish in the ocean, weighing approximately 15 tons (14 metric tons). It has a broad, flat head with a short snout and a long body. The shark's body colorings can range from blue to brown to shades of gray, and the animal has light markings all over. The markings are unique on every whale shark. This helps scientists identify individual whale sharks as the fish migrate.

Despite their huge size, whale sharks are not aggressive, and they even allow divers to swim next to them. Their size also keeps them safe from most predators, though juvenile whale sharks are attacked by blue sharks, blue marlins, and orcas. Whale sharks' tough skin helps protect them from these predators, and researchers have recorded whale sharks with scars and bite marks from surviving these confrontations.

Whale sharks migrate throughout the year. These animals stick to tropical and warm temperate ocean waters throughout the world. They're often seen feeding near the surface, though research shows some whale sharks are able to dive to depths of more than 5,577 feet (1,700 m).[45]

PROTECTING THESE MYSTERIOUS SHARKS

Researchers have never seen a whale shark mate or give birth, and few people have seen baby whale sharks in their natural habitats. "Here is the biggest fish in the oceans. . . . And what is known about their reproductive behavior is almost nothing," said Jonathan R. Green, who directs a whale shark research project in the Galápagos Islands.[46]

Some of what researchers do know comes from dissecting whale sharks. In 1995, a dead female whale shark was found with approximately 300 embryos in her body. The embryos were at different developmental stages. Most were in egg cases with external yolk sacs that they used for food, but some larger ones—with the largest being approximately 2 feet (0.6 m) long—weren't in cases and didn't have yolk sacs, leading researchers to believe the mother was ready to give birth to them. The ranging stages of development made

FUN FACT

In a period of approximately 2.5 years, one whale shark was observed migrating 12,516 miles (20,143 km).[47]

Whale sharks can be found in a handful of large aquariums around the world.

researchers think that females can hold onto sperm for a long period of time and choose to fertilize a certain number of eggs.

The IUCN lists whale sharks as endangered. People hunt whale sharks for their meat and fins. People also harm whale sharks by catching them as bycatch and accidently hitting them with boats. Many governments around the world are taking steps to keep whale sharks safe, including by protecting waters where whale sharks swim.

WHALE SHARK
Rhincodon typus

SIZE
39 feet (12 m) long on average

WEIGHT
15 tons (14 metric tons)

RANGE
Tropical and warm temperate oceans worldwide

HABITAT
Near the surface in open seas and coastal areas

DIET
Plankton, fish, small crustaceans

LIFE SPAN
60–100 years in the wild

YELLOWFIN TUNA

Yellowfin tuna are widely used as a food source.

Yellowfin tuna, along with sharks and small fish, gather in a plankton-rich current in the Pacific Ocean. They weave between each other just below the ocean's surface, and the yellowfin tuna search for small fish to eat. A large school of anchovies catches the attention of the tuna. The anchovies swim together, moving around each other and contorting the school into strange shapes. They do this to protect themselves from the predators that surround them, which they can sense with their lateral line systems.

The anchovies form a large ball near the surface. The yellowfin tuna circle the school and at first appear hesitant to try to break through the ranks of the quickly moving anchovies. Then the yellowfin tuna strike. The swiftness of the attack forces groups of anchovies to break off from the main school, and the tuna are quick to snatch up the stragglers. They hit the school over and over to capture as many anchovies as they can to fill their stomachs.

APPEARANCE, HABITAT, AND BEHAVIOR

Yellowfin tuna have large, torpedo-shaped bodies that can reach up to 7.8 feet (2.4 m) in length. The fish have metallic green-blue backs and white, silvery undersides. The fish get their name from their bright yellow anal and dorsal fins, and they also have a yellow stripe that runs along their sides.

FUN FACT
A yellowfin tuna can swim at up to 50 miles per hour (80 kmh) while chasing after quickly moving prey.[49]

Yellowfin tuna are found throughout the world in subtropical and tropical oceans, often in water temperatures that range from 59 to 88 degrees Fahrenheit (15–31°C). They're usually found swimming in the ocean from the surface to depths of 330 feet (100 m).[48] Yellowfin tuna are a migratory species that can travel long distances in a single year, and their movements are likely correlated with their food needs and spawning habits.

A yellowfin tuna reproduces throughout the year, but reproduction happens most often in the summer. The fish needs the water to be 79 degrees Fahrenheit (26°C) or higher to spawn. A single female can release millions of eggs every year, but few of them will ever reach adulthood. This is because the newly hatched tuna are tiny—almost microscopic—and get eaten by other fish.

Those that survive the larval stage exhibit interesting schooling behaviors. Yellowfin tuna aren't picky about what they group up with and often join fish that are approximately the same size as them. People have observed yellowfins in schools with bigeyes, skipjacks, and other tuna species. Large yellowfin tuna in the eastern Pacific will even school with dolphins.

The fishing industry often targets yellowfin tuna, since many people eat this fish. Also, in the United States, yellowfin tuna is the most popular species that people use for canning. When tuna are swimming at the surface, fishers circle the area with a big net and then pull the net up and into the boat. Then they release their catch by opening the net's bottom and letting the fish fall out. This type of fishing poses a risk to dolphins, sharks, sea turtles, and more, since they can be caught in the net as bycatch.

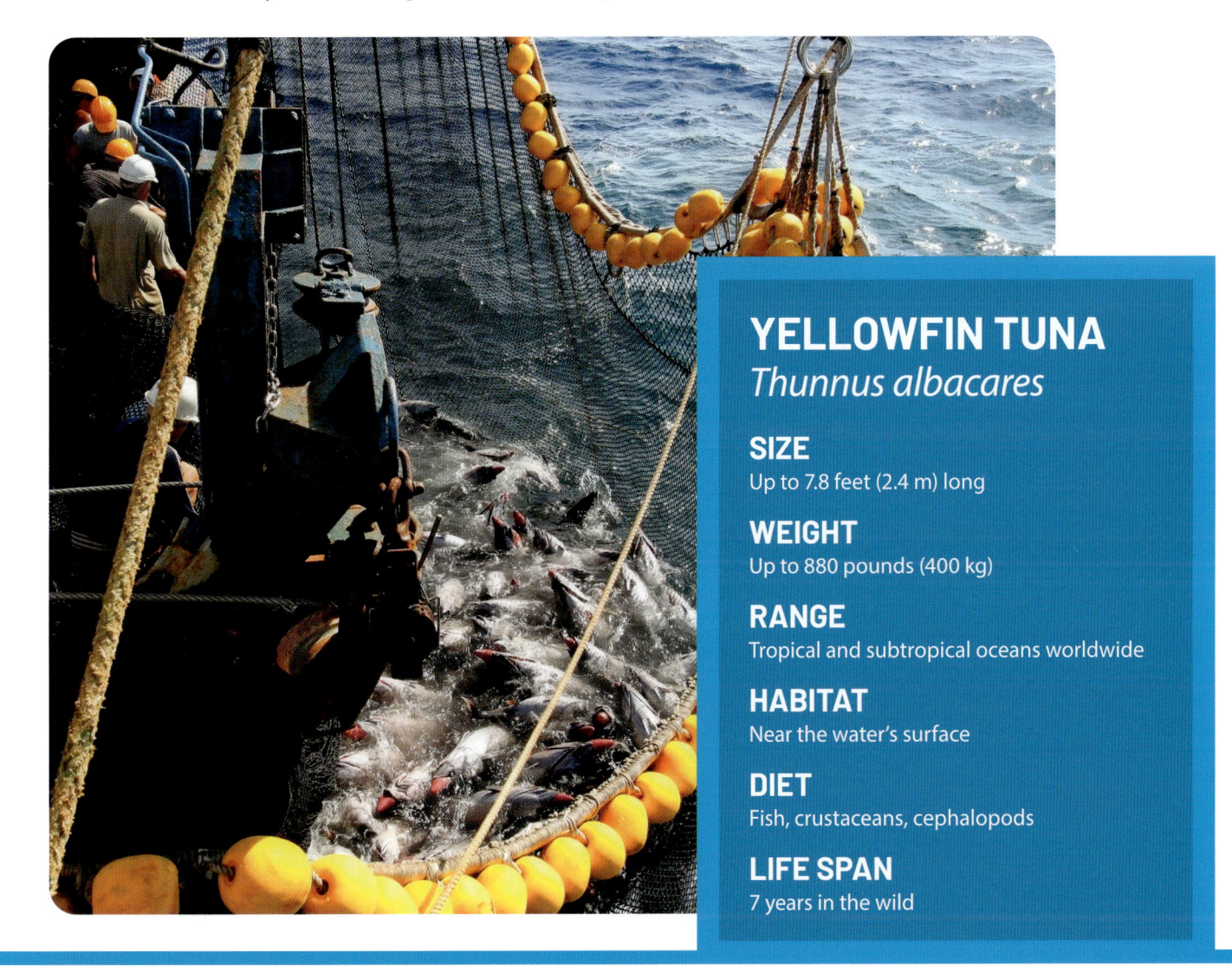

YELLOWFIN TUNA
Thunnus albacares

SIZE
Up to 7.8 feet (2.4 m) long

WEIGHT
Up to 880 pounds (400 kg)

RANGE
Tropical and subtropical oceans worldwide

HABITAT
Near the water's surface

DIET
Fish, crustaceans, cephalopods

LIFE SPAN
7 years in the wild

ESSENTIAL FACTS

FISH FEATURES

- Fish are vertebrates, meaning they have backbones.
- Most fish have gills that help them breathe.
- Many fish have scales that help protect them from certain predators.
- Fish can have different kinds of fins, including dorsal, pectoral, pelvic, anal, and caudal fins.

NOTABLE SPECIES

- The electric eel (*Electrophorus electricus*) has specialized organs that produce electricity, which the fish uses to stun its prey before consuming it.
- The giant manta ray (*Manta birostris*) is the biggest ray in the ocean. It has symbiotic relationships with various fish that pick off dead skin and parasites from the manta ray.
- The great white shark (*Carcharodon carcharias*) is the world's largest predatory fish, and it can smell blood from approximately 3 miles (4.8 km) away.
- During the course of its life, the sockeye salmon (*Oncorhynchus nerka*) lives in both fresh and salt water. It makes an incredible journey from inland bodies of fresh water to the Pacific Ocean and back again.
- The biggest fish in the ocean is the whale shark (*Rhincodon typus*). It is constantly moving and sucking up plankton and small fish to sustain its massive body.

FISH'S ROLES ON EARTH

Fish have served as a food source for humans for thousands of years. These creatures live in fresh and salt water, including in rivers, streams, lakes, ponds, swamps, and oceans. Fish can play various roles in their ecosystems. Sharks serve as top predators and keep fish populations at healthy levels. Other types of fish, such as the Pacific hagfish (*Eptatretus stoutii*), consume dying or dead creatures and keep their ecosystems healthy by recycling nutrients back into the ocean. Some fish, including blue tangs (*Acanthurus coeruleus*), keep coral reefs healthy by picking off algae. Fish such as stingrays help keep the food chain balanced by acting as both predators and prey.

FISH AND CONSERVATION

Both human activities and climate change are threatening some fish species. Pollution can wreak havoc on freshwater and ocean habitats, including by creating toxic algae blooms and destroying coral reefs. Dams and other human-made structures harm fish's traditional migratory patterns and decrease their abilities to spawn. Overfishing can lead to drastic reductions in fish populations. Climate change is hurting a variety of both freshwater and saltwater habitats and making the ocean more acidic.

People are working hard to protect these animals. Conservationists are finding ways to remove human-made structures so fish can return to their traditional spawning grounds. Government officials are protecting threatened fish species by reducing the number of fish that can be caught, and they're also making some water habitats off-limits to activities that can harm fish populations. In addition, organizations, governments, and individuals are trying to slow climate change so diverse fish species throughout the world will continue to provide benefits for their ecosystems for many more generations.

FISH AROUND THE WORLD

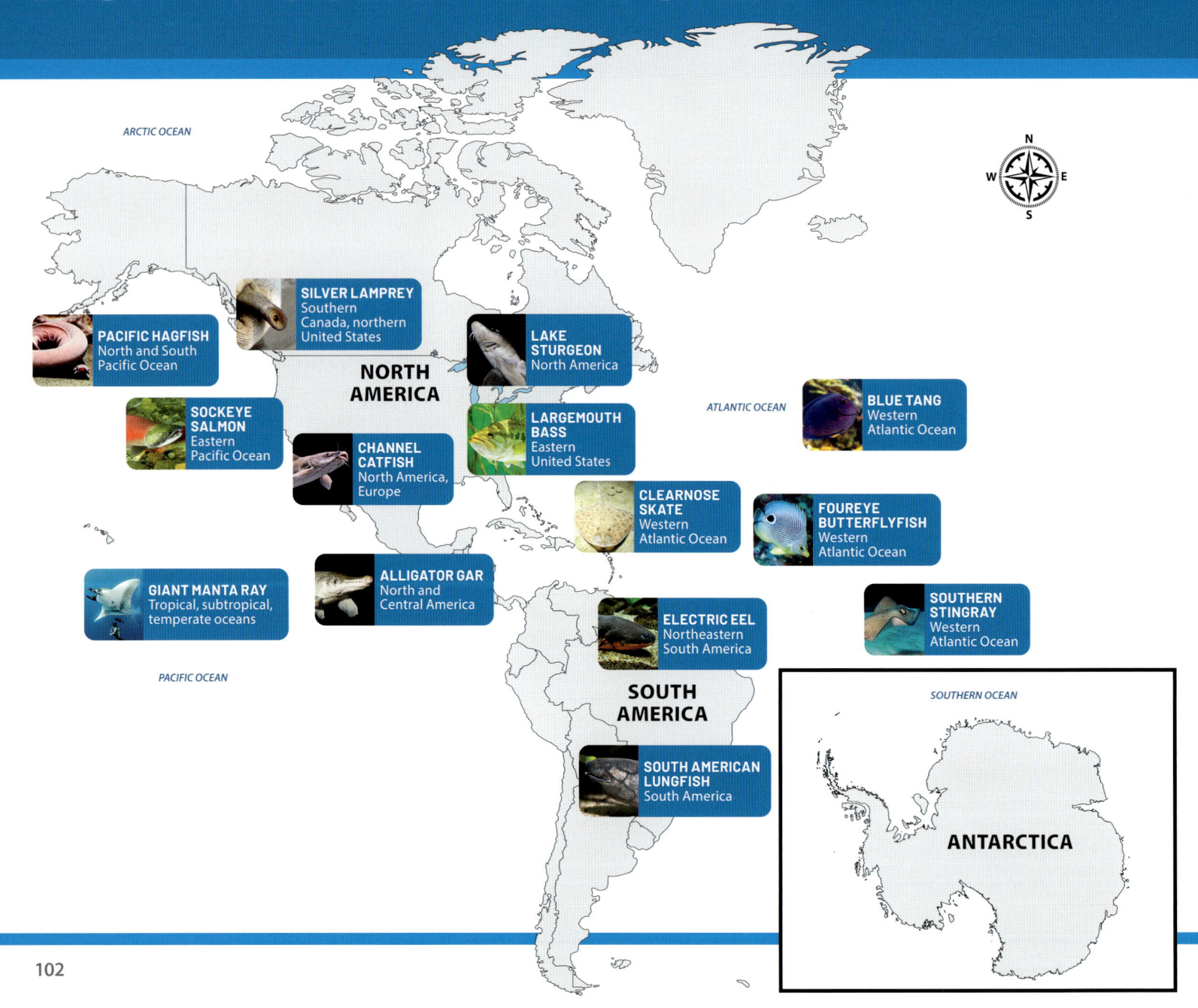

ARCTIC OCEAN

NORTH AMERICA

ATLANTIC OCEAN

PACIFIC OCEAN

SOUTH AMERICA

SOUTHERN OCEAN

ANTARCTICA

PACIFIC HAGFISH
North and South Pacific Ocean

SILVER LAMPREY
Southern Canada, northern United States

LAKE STURGEON
North America

SOCKEYE SALMON
Eastern Pacific Ocean

CHANNEL CATFISH
North America, Europe

LARGEMOUTH BASS
Eastern United States

BLUE TANG
Western Atlantic Ocean

CLEARNOSE SKATE
Western Atlantic Ocean

FOUREYE BUTTERFLYFISH
Western Atlantic Ocean

GIANT MANTA RAY
Tropical, subtropical, temperate oceans

ALLIGATOR GAR
North and Central America

ELECTRIC EEL
Northeastern South America

SOUTHERN STINGRAY
Western Atlantic Ocean

SOUTH AMERICAN LUNGFISH
South America

102

ARCTIC OCEAN

ASIA

EUROPE

SPOT-FIN PORCUPINEFISH
Tropical, subtropical waters

GREAT WHITE SHARK
Temperate oceans

PACIFIC OCEAN

AFRICA

MANDARIN FISH
Western Pacific Ocean

SIAMESE FIGHTING FISH
Thailand

GREAT BARRACUDA
Tropical, subtropical oceans

GRAY REEF SHARK
Indian and Pacific Oceans

YELLOWFIN TUNA
Tropical, subtropical oceans

WHALE SHARK
Tropical, warm temperate oceans

INDIAN OCEAN

ATLANTIC OCEAN

AUSTRALIA

103

GLOSSARY

barbel
A whisker-like organ that helps some fish sense prey.

basin
An area that is drained by a river and smaller waterways.

breed
To reproduce.

bycatch
Animals caught unintentionally by fishers.

caviar
The salted eggs of a big fish.

crustacean
A typically aquatic invertebrate with an exoskeleton and two pairs of antennae; includes crabs, barnacles, and shrimp.

ecosystem
A community of interacting organisms and their environment.

electroreceptor
An organ that can detect an electric field.

estuary
An area where river water meets seawater.

intertidal
Describing an area that is underwater at high tide and above the water at low tide.

mangrove
A shrub or tree with tangled roots near the coast in tropical swamps that flood at high tide.

metabolism
The physical and chemical means by which an organism processes energy.

seamount
A mountain under the sea.

spawn
To deposit or fertilize eggs, often in large numbers.

stagnant
Sitting still; not running or flowing.

subtropical
Bordering a tropical spot.

symbiotic
Mutually beneficial between two or more organisms not of the same species.

temperate
Having mild temperatures.

zooplankton
Microscopic marine animals.

ADDITIONAL RESOURCES

SELECTED BIBLIOGRAPHY

"Fish Groups." *Florida Museum*, n.d., floridamuseum.ufl.edu. Accessed 30 Nov. 2020.

Parenti, Lynne R., and Stanley H. Weitzman. "Fish." *Britannica*, 21 Nov. 2019, britannica.com. Accessed 30 Nov. 2020.

"Threats to Habitat." *NOAA Fisheries*, n.d., fisheries.noaa.gov. Accessed 30 Nov. 2020.

FURTHER READINGS

Blohm, Craig E. *What Is the Impact of Ocean Pollution?* ReferencePoint, 2020.

Hand, Carol. *Bringing Back Our Oceans*. Abdo, 2018.

Hand, Carol. *The Evolution of Fish*. Abdo, 2019.

ONLINE RESOURCES

Booklinks NONFICTION NETWORK
FREE! ONLINE NONFICTION RESOURCES

To learn more about fish, please visit **abdobooklinks.com** or scan this QR code. These links are routinely monitored and updated to provide the most current information available.

MORE INFORMATION

For more information on this subject, contact or visit the following organizations:

National Resources Defense Council
40 W. Twentieth St., Eleventh Floor
New York, NY 10011
212-727-2700
nrdc.org

The National Resources Defense Council is a nonprofit organization. It aims to protect the environment, and its areas of focus include slowing climate change, protecting oceans, and providing clean water to communities.

NOAA Fisheries
1315 East-West Hwy.
Silver Spring, MD 20910
fisheries.noaa.gov

NOAA Fisheries is a US government organization that works to protect the oceans. It provides guidance for sustainable and productive fishing, helps with recovery efforts, and strives to maintain healthy ecosystems for the ocean's many animals.

SOURCE NOTES

1. "About Fish." *National Geographic*, n.d., nationalgeographic.com. Accessed 15 Feb. 2021.

2. Stanley H. Weitzman. "Fish." *Britannica*, 2019, britannica.com. Accessed 15 Feb. 2021.

3. Ann Gibbons. "The World's First Fish Supper." *Science*, 1 June 2010, sciencemag.org. Accessed 15 Feb. 2021.

4. Ronald Strahan. "Agnathan." *Britannica*, 2019, britannica.com. Accessed 15 Feb. 2021.

5. "Vertebrate Diversity." *UCL*, n.d., ucl.ac.uk. Accessed 15 Feb. 2021.

6. "Vertebrate Diversity."

7. "Fish Groups." *Florida Museum*, 14 July 2020, floridamuseum.ufl.edu. Accessed 15 Feb.2021.

8. "About Fish."

9. Casey McGrath. "Highlight: Big Surprises from the World's Smallest Fish." *Genome Biol. Evol.*, 12 Apr. 2018, ncbi.nlm.nih.gov. Accessed 15 Feb. 2021.

10. "Whale Shark." *Britannica*, 2020, britannica.com. Accessed 15 Feb. 2021.

11. "Alligator Gar." *National Geographic*, n.d., nationalgeographic.com. Accessed 15 Feb. 2021.

12. Genna Woodruff. "Acanthurus Coeruleus." *Animal Diversity Web*, 2006, animaldiversity.org. Accessed 15 Feb. 2021.

13. "Channel Catfish." *Smithsonian's National Zoo*, n.d., nationalzoo.si.edu. Accessed 15 Feb. 2021.

14. Molly Miller. "Raja Eglanteria." *Animal Diversity Web*, 2013, animaldiversity.org. Accessed 15 Feb. 2021.

15. "Raja Eglanteria." *Florida Museum*, 30 Apr. 2018, floridamuseum.ufl.edu. Accessed 15 Feb. 2021.

16. "Electric Eel." *Smithsonian's National Zoo*, n.d., nationalzoo.si.edu. Accessed 15 Feb. 2021.

17. "Electric Eel."

18. "Electric Eel."

19. "Chaetodon Capistratus." *Online Guide to the Animals of Trinidad and Tobago*, n.d., sta.uwi.edu. Accessed 15 Feb. 2021.

20. Patrick L. Colin. "Aspects of the Spawning of Western Atlantic Butterflyfishes." *Environmental Biology of Fishes*, 1989, link.springer.com. Accessed 15 Feb. 2021.

21. Gregory Shuraleff II, "Manta Birostris." *Animal Diversity Web*, 2000, animaldiversity.org. Accessed 15 Feb. 2021.

22. "Manta Birostris." *Florida Museum*, n.d., floridamuseum.ufl.edu. Accessed 15 Feb. 2021.

23. "Sphyraena Barracuda." *Florida Museum*, n.d., floridamuseum.ufl.edu. Accessed 15 Feb. 2021.

24. "Sphyraena Barracuda."

25. "Breaching Great White Shark on the Hunt." *Smithsonian Ocean*, n.d., ocean.si.edu. Accessed 15 Feb. 2021.

26. Ki Mae Heussner. "Expedition Great White: Catching the Ocean's Largest Predatory Fish." *ABC News*, 13 Nov. 2009, abcnews.go.com. Accessed 15 Feb. 2021.

27. "Yearly Worldwide Shark Attack Summary." *Florida Museum*, 27 Jan. 2021, floridamuseum.ufl.edu. Accessed 15 Feb. 2021.

28. Emma Rigney. "Orcas Eat Great White Sharks—New Insights into Rare Behavior Revealed." *National Geographic*, 16 July 2019, nhm.org. Accessed 15 Feb. 2021.

29. Jennifer Hile. "Great White Shark Attacks: Defanging the Myths." *National Geographic*, 23 Jan. 2004, nationalgeographic.com. Accessed 15 Feb. 2021.

30. Ben Finley, Patrick Whittle, and John Flesher. "Sturgeon, America's Forgotten Dinosaurs, Slowly Coming Back." *AP News*, 10 July 2019, apnews.com. Accessed 15 Feb. 2021.

31. "Lake Sturgeon." *US Fish and Wildlife Service*, 9 Jan. 2020, fws.gov. Accessed 15 Feb. 2021.

32. Emily Steed. "Micropterus Salmoides." *Animal Diversity Web*, 2018, animaldiversity.org. Accessed 15 Feb. 2021.

33. Steed, "Micropterus Salmoides."

34. "Mandarin Dragonet Fish Facts and Care." *Pet Helpful*, 13 Aug. 2019, pethelpful.com. Accessed 15 Feb. 2021.

35. Brett Schroeder. "Eptatretus Stoutii." *Animal Diversity Web*, 2006, animaldiversity.org. Accessed 15 Feb. 2021.

36. Hannah Waters. "14 Fun Facts about Hagfish." *Smithsonian*, 17 Oct. 2012, smithsonianmag.com. Accessed 15 Feb. 2021.

37. "Pacific Hagfish." *Aquarium of the Pacific*, n.d., aquariumofpacific.org. Accessed 15 Feb. 2021.

38. Philip A. Purser. "Better Betta-Keeping." *Tropical Fish Hobbyist Magazine*, Apr. 2007, tfhmagazine.com. Accessed 29 Mar. 2021.

39. Chelsea Blumbergs. "Ichthyomyzon Unicuspis." *Animal Diversity Web*, 2014, animaldiversity.org. Accessed 15 Feb. 2021.

40. "Sea Lamprey." *Great Lakes Fishery Commission*, n.d., glfc.org. Accessed 15 Feb. 2021.

41. Ocean Wise. "The Epic Journey—Follow a Salmon from Egg to Spawner." *YouTube*, 19 Oct. 2018, youtube.com. Accessed 15 Feb. 2021.

42. "Sockeye Salmon." *NOAA Fisheries*, n.d., fisheries.noaa.gov. Accessed 15 Feb. 2021.

43. Stephanie Elliott. "Lepidosiren Paradoxa." *Animal Diversity Web*, 2005, animaldiversity.org. Accessed 15 Feb. 2021.

44. Ivana Pavic. "Dasyatis Americana." *Animal Diversity Web*, 2012, animaldiversity.org. Accessed 15 Feb. 2021.

45. Paulina Calleros and Jessica Vazquez. "Rhincodon Typus." *Animal Diversity Web*, 2012, animaldiversity.org. Accessed 15 Feb. 2021.

46. Ashifa Kassam. "The Ocean's Largest Mystery—Why Has No One Seen a Whale Shark Give Birth?" *Guardian*, 9 July 2020, theguardian.com. Accessed 15 Feb. 2021.

47. "Longest Recorded Whale Shark Migration Eclipses 20,000 Kilometers." *Mongabay*, 14 May 2018, news.mongabay.com. Accessed 15 Feb. 2021.

48. "Thunnus Albacares." *Fishbase*, n.d., fishbase.in. Accessed 15 Feb. 2021.

49. Anne Marie Helmenstine, PhD. "Yellowfin Tuna Facts." *ThoughtCo*, 13 Mar. 2019, thoughtco.com. Accessed 15 Feb. 2021.

INDEX

Africa, 37, 48, 59
Amazon River, 31, 83
anchovies, 96–97
aquariums, 5, 62–63, 71
Asia, 11, 14
Atlantic Ocean, 19, 25, 27, 35, 45, 46, 57, 75, 86, 87, 88, 90

balloonfish, 91
barbels, 22, 52–53, 64
barracudas, 44–47
bass, 56–59, 74
birds, 59, 62, 86

catfish, 6, 20–23, 74
Central America, 14, 15
classification of fish, 5–7
coral reefs, 9–10, 11, 16–17, 19, 32–33, 35, 40, 42, 43, 46, 47, 60–62, 63, 88
crustaceans, 14, 63, 84, 87, 95, 99

dams, 11, 14, 55
defense mechanisms, 16–17, 22, 29, 32–33, 61, 65–67, 85, 89
dolphins, 98–99

eels, 28–31, 33, 72
egg capsules, 26–27
eggs, 15, 18, 20, 30, 34, 55, 57, 61, 67, 69, 73, 77, 83, 91, 94
Europe, 14, 59
evolution, 7, 67

farming, 23
Finding Nemo, 17
fins, 8
fishing, 55, 98–99
fossils, 4, 6, 14, 67

gars, 12–15
gills, 4, 6, 30, 37, 65, 78, 82, 85, 92
Great Lakes, 6, 53, 55, 57, 73, 75
Green, Jonathan R., 94
groupers, 16–17, 46
Gulf of Mexico, 14, 26, 27, 32, 37, 45, 86, 87

hagfish, 6, 11, 64–67

Indian Ocean, 40, 42, 90
International Union for the Conservation of Nature (IUCN), 43, 95
invasive species, 75
invertebrates, 23, 32, 35, 67, 82, 83

Klimley, A. Peter, 51

lampreys, 6, 22, 53, 72–75, 78
live young, 4, 43
lungfish, 80–83

marlins, 93
Mediterranean Sea, 90
Mighall, Hannah, 51
migration, 11, 26, 93, 94, 97
Miller, Jeff, 54
Munroe, Tom, 67

noodling, 22–23
North America, 13, 14, 15, 21, 22, 53, 55, 77, 79

orcas, 50, 93
overfishing, 14, 43, 55

Pacific Ocean, 43, 46, 47, 60–63, 65, 67, 76–79, 90, 96
plankton, 34, 37, 39, 78, 79, 92, 95, 96
poison, 14, 61, 89
pollution, 10
porcupinefish, 88–91

rays, 6, 9, 26, 36–39, 84–87
relationship to humans, 4–5
remora fish, 39
rivers, 4, 9, 11, 12, 14, 15, 21, 23, 28, 31, 53, 55, 57, 59, 73–75, 76–78, 83

salmon, 76–79
scales, 4, 6, 13, 22, 34, 61, 65, 69, 89
schools, 4, 19, 37, 40, 45, 93, 96–97, 98
scientists, 4–5, 14, 15, 18, 26, 31, 38, 51, 67, 83, 90, 91, 93, 94–95

seals, 48–49, 65, 78
sense organs, 9, 22, 28–30, 52, 64, 82, 96
sharks, 6, 9, 11, 26, 38, 40–43, 46, 48–51, 78, 85, 92–95, 96, 99
skates, 6, 9, 24–27
South America, 31, 80, 82–83
spawning, 11, 15, 18, 55, 56, 72–73, 77–79, 97
sturgeon, 6, 52–55, 72–73, 74
swim bladders, 8, 13, 82

tangs, 11, 16–19
Thailand, 50, 70, 71
tuna, 6, 46, 96–99

United States, 14, 15, 23, 57, 58, 59, 71, 75, 98

wrasses, 39, 86

111

ABOUT THE AUTHOR
Alyssa Krekelberg

Alyssa Krekelberg lives in Minnesota with her husband and their hyper husky. When she's not writing books, Alyssa works as an editor and especially enjoys projects that focus on the environment and what people can do to protect it.

ABOUT THE CONSULTANT
Dr. Jessica Arbour

Dr. Jessica Arbour is a professor of biology at Middle Tennessee State University. She is interested in how different groups of fish have evolved and has named two species of fish from South America. When not conducting research on fish, Dr. Arbour enjoys working on her tropical freshwater aquariums, folding origami, playing video games, and spending time with her husband and fluffy dog.